Isabella La

# THE MEDICI VILLAS

## COMPLETE GUIDE

*With a text by Mario Scalini*

**GIUNTI** FIRENZE MVSEI

*Project and editorial coordination*
Claudio Pescio
*Graphics*
Giovanni Breschi
*Page format*
Paola Zacchini
*Translation*
Michael Sullivan, Eleonor Daunt for NTL
*Editing of the english translation*
Giorgio Bizzi
*Visitors' informations*
Chiara Senesi
*Maps*
Legenda, Novara / Sergio Biagi
*Photolithograph*
Fotolito Toscana

*Photographs references*
Archivio Giunti; Archivio Giunti/Foto Nicola
Grifoni; Archivio Soprintendenza per i Beni
Ambientali e Architettonici, Firenze;
Giovanni Breschi; Isabella Lapi Ballerini;
Antonio Quattrone

The author wishes to thank the owners e
the managments of the villas shown in this
volume, either public than private, for
their kind cooperation.

www.giunti.it

ISBN 8809-02-995X

Realizzazione di Giunti Gruppo Editoriale,
Firenze

Prima edizione: aprile 2003

| Ristampa | | | | | | Anno | | | |
|---|---|---|---|---|---|---|---|---|---|
| 6 | 5 | 4 | 3 | 2 | 1 | 2006 | 2005 | 2004 | 2003 |

Stampato presso
Giunti Industrie Grafiche S.p.A.
Stabilimento di Prato

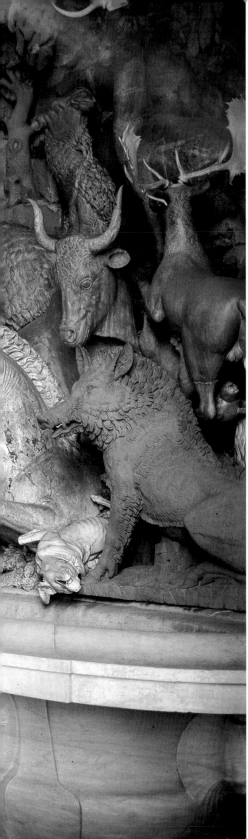

# Contents

Introduction by                                          7
*Antonio Paolucci*

Between the history of yesterday                          8
and the museum of today

THE MEDICI VILLAS IN THE FLORENTINE
MUSEUM SYSTEM

Villa della Petraia                                      16
Villa di Castello                                        30
Villa di Poggio a Caiano                                 42
Villa di Cerreto Guidi (*Mario Scalini*)                 58

OTHER MEDICI VILLAS IN TUSCANY

Villa del Trebbio                                        68
Villa di Cafaggiolo                                      71
Villa di Careggi                                         75
Villa Medici in Fiesole                                 78
Villa di Collesalvetti                                  82
Villa di Agnano                                          83
Villa di Spedaletto                                      84
Villa di Camugliano                                      86
Villa La Topaia                                          90
Villa di Seravezza                                       92
Villa di Stabbia                                         94
Villa di Pratolino                                       95
Villa di Lappeggi                                       100
Villa di Marignolle                                    103
Villa La Magia                                          105
Villa di Coltano                                        107
Villa dell'Ambrogiana                                  110
Villa di Artimino                                       114
Villa di Montevettolini                                117
Villa di Poggio Imperiale                              119

Index of names                                         122

Bibliographic references                               125

*NOTE*
The order by which the "other villas" are
shown in the present volume is in accordance
with the chronology by which they went
under possession of the Medici family

At the pages 2-3
Villa di Poggio a Caiano

Beside,
a detail of the 'Grotto of the Animals'
in the garden of Castello

The recent change to main and branch offices of the Amministrazione dei Beni Culturali has assigned the Medici Villas still in the ownership of the state (La Petraia, Poggio a Caiano, Giardino di Castello, Cerreto Guidi) to the Polo Museale Fiorentino; the newly instituted Soprintendenza Speciale autonomous. It was not easy to get to the government bill (Decreto Ministeriale of 26/06/2002) defining this necessary aggregation. The initial decision was different. The Medici Villas were excluded from the museum department of the Polo. It took my own determination and that of General Director Mario Serio and the wisdom of Minister Giuliano Urbani to ensure the rectification came in a reasonably short time.

So now the Medici Villas spoken of by Isabella Lapi Ballerini and Mario Scalini in the book my lines introduce are entrusted to the Office that governs the great Florentine museums and the Reggia di Pitti. It is a revindication that renews the old arrangement. In certain sense it reconciles the Villas with their history. Because the Crown residences were nothing less than the Royal Palace transferred into the country . For centuries they maintained an osmotic relation with the Royal Palace of exchange and reflection, they were lived in by the same people, governed by an equal logic of administration, use, collecting. Then came the nineteenth century with the resignations and the scattering, then the twentieth century with its specialisations and its artificial bureaucratic partitions. The Crown residences that belonged to the state were entrusted till recently to the Soprintendenza ai Beni Ambientali e Architettonici because they were considered more monument than places of dynastic collectionism.

Now – I repeat – the hacked-off limb has been sewn back. The villas are once again an integral part of the grand-ducal 'system' of collecting that the old Soprintendenza alle Gallerie (now Polo Museale autonomous) is called upon to govern.

Convinced as we are that Good Government starts from good knowledge and good divulgation of knowledge, the first act of the new administrative regime could only be this: an official guide, published by Giunti top of the list for the Concessionaria that has in keeping the museums of the Polo in adherence to the Ronchey Law.

The guide is edited by Isabella Lapi Ballerini and Mario Scalini; the former director of the Petraia, of the Giardino di Castello, of Poggio a Caiano, the latter of Cerreto Guidi. The result is thus the best we might have hoped in terms of historical synthesis and technico-scholarly trustworthiness. The guide photographs the situation of the villas in the spring of 2003. Everything we shall do from now on (and we want to do a great deal in terms of restoration, regularisation, optimisation, new arrangements) we shall do from the starting-point of the pages of this book.

*Antonio Paolucci*
*Superintendent for Polo Museale Fiorentino*

Jacopo Pontormo
*Vertumnus and Pomona,*
c. 1519-1520, detail;
Villa di Poggio a Caiano

# Between the history of yesterday and the museum of today

When the Fleming Justus Utens painted the series of lunettes showing the *Medici Villas* for Ferdinando I, that were then hung in the Villa di Artimino, the fortunes of the Medici family were at their peak of splendour. The spread of properties stretched from Mugello to the plain of the Arno towards Pisa and Leghorn, shaped like a sort of fan open to the north-west in terms of Florence. At the close of the 16th century the painter diligently recorded a situation that, without his knowing it, was and to remain unchanged, apart from minimal additions or subtractions, down to the ending of the ruling line in 1737. So, the land sytem of the Medici villas – and not only of those shown by Artimino in his iconographical summary – was all definined already, and identified with the consolidated power of the dynasty.

In the three centuries of their historical sway the Medici busied themselves with increasing, enlarging, conquering, building, endowing, collecting. The villas reflect the evolution of all this extrordinary work of aggregation that led Florence to control the balance of Europe. All characterized by their nature of country residence immersed in the landscape, they took on shape by harmoniously changing form and function according to the wishes and the tastes of the various patrons. In the first place rural alternatives to the toils and political life of the city ("How blessed it will be staying in a country villa: an unknown happiness!", wrote Leon Battista Alberti), but also, if need be, a safe refuge guaranteed by an independent productivity that they were to maintained for the whole fifteenth century (Trebbio, Cafaggiolo, Careggi, Fiesole, Poggio a Caiano), by being villa-farms where farming activity was dominant (Collesalvetti, Spedaletto, Agnano, Coltano), they were to become with the birth of the grand-duchy the visible and formidable sign of the presence of the Prince in his fief.

The sign was now shaped to the measure of grandeur (the architecture and ornaments), of politics (the strategic location), but even of enthusiasms (hunting). While the transformation from Renaissance city-state to territorial principate was taking place, interest in farming and villa life took new form. Through worked-out programmes, that involved architects, engineers, men of letters and artists, the villas and the sur-

Giorgio Vasari
*Portrait of Lorenzo de' Medici*, 1534;
Florence, Uffizi

8

rounding areas became the centres for invention, technologies, marvels and rarities, that were at bottom nothing less than dreams of the infinite. Thus at a pace that was to increase from the rise of Cosimo I in the fourth decade of the 16<sup>th</sup> century and go on under his sons Francesco and Ferdinando for more than half a century, the scenographich allegories of the Giardino di Castello were created, a model of political propaganda then copied throughout Europe, the basis was laid for the control of resources, such as marble and the silver of Seravezza, or of commercial arteries, like the Arno in the case of Ambrogiana, comfort, decked out with botanical delights, as at Petraia, was simply sought for, the hunting season and the health of the climate was pursued, sometimes allowing oneself the pure pleasure of luxury and the magnificence that everyone recognised, as soon as it was completed by Francesco I, in Pratolino.

Giambologna
*Cosimo I de' Medici,*
after 1546, detail;
Florence, Uffizi

The indirect protagonist of the operation was always, as one can well understand in looking at Utens' lunettes, the unmistakable and lenient Tuscan countryside. The villas in fact shaped, with or without the ornate mediation of the garden, a new network of relationships with the surrounding landscape, which in its turn flowed back on them reconstructed in the form of roadways, in the partitioning of crops, in the 'wilderness' of the thick woods populated by every kind of animals. This was the case with the reclamation and channeling of the waters controlled by villas of Valdinievole and of the area of Fucecchio, or of the grandiose Medici Barco reale on Mount Albano, a hunting reserve of ten thousand acres enclosed by a wall thirty miles long, begun by Lorenzo the Magnificent but enlarged mainly by Cosimo I and Ferdinando I, in a short time surrounded by a quantity of satellite villas.

Of this symbolic universe Artimino, the commanding and austere 'Ferdinanda', became the conceptual centre, perfect envelope for the record of family properties scrupulously transcribed by Justus Utens. Thanks to the "spreading view of country" made possible by the hill chosen by Ferdinando for its construction, Artimino appears as the terrace *par excellence* from which the Prince might look out on his grand-duchy, surrounded by the court, at the summit of absolutism. When the purpose of celebration faded during the course of the 17<sup>th</sup> century, the Medici Villas increasingly served logistical functions as resting places in the continual transfers of the court, or residential ones, with embellishments that followed the taste of the different inhabitants, or of pleasure, for those members of the Medici house, and they were not few, inclined to luxury and revels, such as cardinals Giovan Carlo at Careggi and Castello and Francesco Maria at Lappeggi. Patronage, less grandiose but always present, was to evolve into a form of collecting at times culti-

Domenico Poggini
*Francesco I
de' Medici,*
before 1564, detail;
Florence, Uffizi

Florentine painter
from the circle
of Alessandro
Allori,
*The cardinal
and grand-duke
Ferdinando I
de' Medici,*
after 1588, detail;
Florence, Uffizi,
Depositi

Baldassarre
Franceschini,
known as
Il Volterrano,
*Portrait of Giovan
Carlo de' Medici,*
after 1563, detail;
Florence,
Galleria Palatina

vated at times curious. This was the case with Don Lorenzo at Petraia, who gave us the masterpiece by Baldassarre Franceschini, know as Il Volterrano, or with the paintings of plants and animal gathered by Cosimo III at Topaia and Ambrogiana, or with the talent for display of Grand Prince Ferdinando who in Poggio at Caiano hung as many as one hundred and seventy-four paintings in a single room!

All this patrimony, destined to follow in good and evil the dynasties ruling Tuscany, was, with the coming in of the Lorraine, dismembered in terms of estates and buildings and, as for the collections, largely piled together without any criterion. When the concept of representativity had faded, felt often as a useless burden on the finances of the state, their splendour – or rather their melancholy beauty by then – misunderstood as the product of an aesthetising ideology, the villas succumbed to the utilitarian philosophy govered by 'reason' proper to the culture of the Enlightenment. A process of condemnation and denial that, after the sale of the greater part of landed property by the Lorraine administration in 1782, and after the losses during the Napoleonic interlude, was to culminate in the tragic demolition of the 'marvellous' Pratolino, an act perpetrated by Ferdinando III at the start of the 19th century.

With the Unification of Italy the image of the Medici villas was to be strongly marked by the work of adaptation to the needs and taste of the new sovereigns and above all by the rearranging of the furnishings, consequent on the great quantity of furniture and art objects from all over the country that became Crown property. Since then, after alternating moments of cession and re-appropriations, the greater part privatised and destined to other improper or ill-fitting uses, as in the case of the criminal asylum at Ambrogiana or the hospital offices at Careggi, the image of what the Medici villas were is now concentrated in the few belonging to the state and transformed into museums. The Villas of Poggio a Caiano and of the Petraia, the Garden of the Villa di Castello, the Villa of Cerreto Guidi which, sold in

1780, was restored to public enjoyment in 1969 thanks to the far-sightedness of a private donor, enclose within their confines the task of handing on memories, the power to evoke them, the energies to preserve them and make them feel alive and relevant. If the primary task of us curators or directors is now, after considerable debate on the issue, that of preserving their appearance when they were last used in time, that is under the royals of the House of Savoy, there is also the need to make the most of them, to reconstitute displays, and serve educational needs, by filling the empty spaces or by making good eventual damage on the margin of what these villas should be, before anything else, museum of themselves.

In prepararing this guide which, by publishing choice, is devoted in the first place to the museums of the Medici villas, but also aims at being a complete guide to the others, it was decided to include those in which the Medici played a fundamental role in construction or evolution, while remaining aware of how many others were administered, for some time or in some way, by members of that great family, such as La Quiete, Mezzomonte or like many farms and hunting-lodges it would be too long to list.

Of those drawn out of the dimness resulting from dispersal and oblivion a brief chronology is offered, in the aim of recreating a virtual image of what the villas meant to the Medici over the course of time. Starting from these notes, fragments of a variegated history, we hope that reader will then find the leading thread in the museums of the Medici villas that through a more kindly fate can be visited today and are within reach of everybody.

Aware that the legacy of art, of furnishings and memories they safeguard will always be able to offer the alert visitor, who chooses to leave the beaten track of city museums, a vision unique in the world.

Justus Sustermans,
*Portrait
of Cosimo III,*
c. 1660, detail;
Florence,
Galleria Palatina

Niccolò Cassani,
*The Grand Prince
Ferdinando
de' Medici,*
c. 1687, detail;
Florence, Uffizi,
Vasari Corridor

*I. L. B.*
*February 2003*

11

1 Villa La Topaia

2 Villa della Petraia

3 Villa di Castello

4 Villa di Poggio
  a Caiano

5 Villa di Careggi

6 Villa di Pratolino

7 Villa Medici in Fiesole

8 Villa di Lappeggi

9 Villa di Poggio
  Imperiale

10 Villa di Marignolle

11 Villa di Artimino

# The Medici Villas in the outskirts of Florence

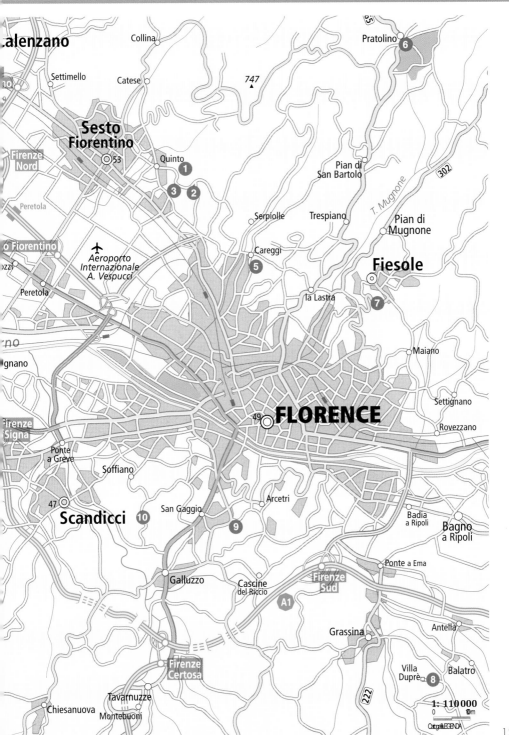

1 Villa del Trebbio

2 Villa di Cafaggiolo

3 Villa La Magia

4 Villa di Montevettolini

5 Villa di Stabbia

6 Villa di Cerreto Guidi

7 Villa dell'Ambrogiana

8 Villa di Spedaletto

9 Villa di Camugliano

10 Villa di Collesalvetti

11 Villa di Coltano

12 Villa di Agnano

13 Villa di Seravezza

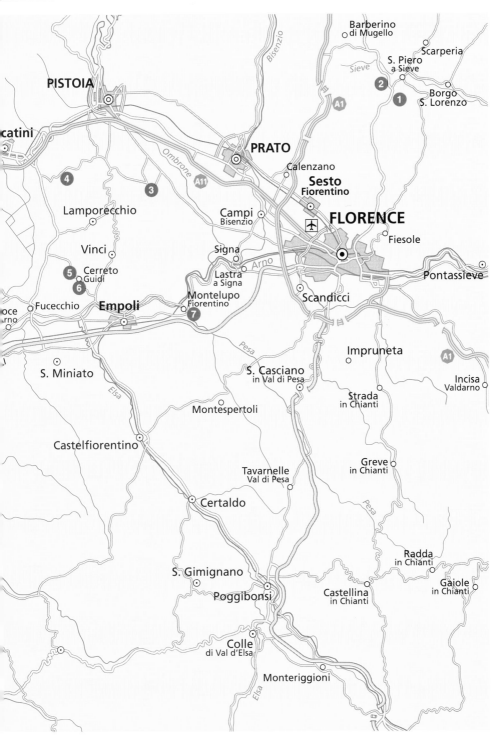

# Villa della Petraia

Its happy position in the landscape, the excellence of the painted decorations, the stimulating blend of forms and styles, the lush nature of the park, make the Petraia one of the most charming of Medici villas. An ancient fortified 'palagio', from the which the Brunelleschi family managed to repel the siege by the Pisan troops under Giovanni Acuto in 1364, later belonging in to the wealthy merchant Palla Strozzi and to the Salutati, it was bought in 1544 by Cosimo I de' Medici. The early work of restructuring, entrusted by the Duke to Davide Fortini in 1566, was broken off almost immediately, after the building was given in 1568 to his son cardinal Ferdinando, at the time busy to Rome where he was living in the unfinished Palazzo Florence and the grandiose Villa Medici on the Pincio. Named Grand-duke in October 1587, after

## HOW TO GET THERE

At Castello,
between Sesto Fiorentino and Careggi.
*Address* via di Petraia 40,
Castello (Florence).
*Bus* 2, 28
*Tel* +39 055 452691
*Opening times* (tickets sale stops 1 1/2 h before closing time) 8:15-17:00 (Nov thru Feb); 8:15-18 (March); 8:15-19 (Apr, May, Sep, Oct); 8:15-20 (Jun-Aug). Closed the second and third Monday of the month.
*Entry* € 2.00 (full); € 1.00 (reduced). The ticket also covers a visit to the park of Villa Medici di Castello if made on the same day.
Guided tour inside.

the sudden death of his brother Francesco, Ferdinando devoted himself to the transforming, already begun by his father, of a primitive 'gentleman's house' into a residence worthy of a prince. Great quantities of earth were moved over the decade beginning 1588, enough to transform the 'stony' place into a scenic sequence of terraces dominated by the compact bulk of the villa. Thus a new and important element was added to the process

ence he had gained in laying out the splendid garden on the Pincio was exploited by Ferdinando for the three levels in which the 'walled' garden was divided. As one sees in Utens's painting, the level of the villa, cut off above by the 'wilderness', was enriched on the two sides by dwarf orchards, the true rarity of the sixteenth-century garden; the nursery level below, occupied by the large reservoir, held the flower and 'simple' garden (medicinal

LA PRETAIA

of robust architectural affirmation of dynastic power which Utens shortly afterwards recorded in the calligraphic lunettes of the *Ville Medici* painted for Artimino. The novelty came rather from the garden than the architecture of the villa. If the latter, traditionally attributed to Buontalenti though the only sure thing is that Raffaello Pagni was there, underwent rearrangement according to canonical forms within the primitive watchtower, the formal and botanical experi-

plants), divided in elaborate geometrical designs; the lower slope featured two ellipses, which, cut off by 'cerchiate' (pergolas) of evergreens, were subdivided into beds with fruit trees; there was no lack of citrus fruit in vases and orange trees espaliered up the boundary wall, a necessary feature of every princely garden. The features that distinguished the new residence, situated in an area (the "bank" of Castello) famous from antiquity for the softness of the landscape and for the abundance of its waters, look shaped to the needs of everyday life, to be enjoyed in the quiet of this ideal terrace looking down onto the plain below, rather than for the purpose of display entrusted to the various artistic allegories as with Castello, or the mainly hunting purpose of the numerous villas with which Ferdinando was to stud the perimeter of Monte Albano. This explains the attention given to the vegetation and functional aspects of the garden, without sculptures or fountains, and the sober simplicity of the building, that at the time contained just one exceptional work, the *Bruto* by Michelangelo. Among the few experiments at decoration was that by Ferdinando's wife Cristina of Lorraine, to whom the villa was assigned after their wedding in 1589: the frescoes on the theme of the Sacred in the Cappella Vecchia on the first floor are the work of Bernardino Poccetti helped by the little known Cosimo Daddi, and, in honour of the illustrious Lorraine ancestor of the Grand-duchess, the *Exploits of Goffredo of Buglion at the taking of Jerusalem*, painted by Daddi on two walls of the courtyard. Their son Don Lorenzo, who inherited in 1609, was responsible for enriching the villa with a cycle of paintings that not is not just a celebration of the family but also a masterpiece painting, the *Fasti Medicei*. Painted by Baldassarre Franceschini, know as Il Volterrano, under the loggias of the courtyard (1637-1646), with scenes conceived as grandiose banners of a triumphal parade, confer a magnificence on the country residence worthy of the Salone di Giovanni da San Giovanni in Palazzo Pitti and of the older *Scene storiche* in the 'Leo X Room' in Poggio a Caiano. After the refined Don Lorenzo, who also

brought together a choice selection of paintings there, and after the decoration of the Cappella Nuova, decided on by Cosimo III, with frescoes by Pier Dandini and Rinaldo Botti (c. 1696), the Petraia failed

to interest the 'late Medici', who indeed gradually stripped it, to the point that the Prince of Craon, who lived there during his regency after the coming of the Lorraine (1737), found it as sadly empty. Under the new Grand-dukes, it was variations in wall coverings or furniture, frequently removed from one residence to another, according to the tastes and the needs of the different owners, that characterised the interior of the villa. Thus we find the Games Room, a unique exam-

The fountain on the Piano della Figurina, with the *Venus-Florence* (or *Fiorenza*) by Giambologna (1570-1572)

ple of its kind, furnished with odd evidence of a period inclined to pastimes; or the fine collection of Chinese watercolours, bought by Pietro Leopoldo towards 1785 following the vogue for 'chinoiserie', among which stands out, beside the small paintings on the typical themes of rice, silk, porcelain and tea, an extremely rare *View of the port of Canton* done in gouache on a silk scroll. Objects often of great refinement are nonchalantly mismatched in most of the rooms with the ordinary wallpaper (*papier peints*) that had spread by then from France to all Europe. The most significant changes, however, involved the garden and the park. In 1788 the *Fountain of Florence* (or *Fiorenza*) was moved from Villa di Castello to the east garden of the Petraia, known since then as Piano della Figurina from the famous sculpture of *Venus-Florence* (or *Fiorenza*) by Giambologna that crowns it. From 1829, by the wishes of Leopoldo II, the vast romantic park to the north of the villa replaced the 'wilderness' and the sixteenth-century netting sheds. It was laid out with mitteleuropean taste by the bohemian gardener Joseph Frietsch, who a few years earlier had designed for Ferdinando III the Pratolino park; the carriageway linking the two villas was built in the same period (1833). With the Unification of Italy, and with the transfer of the capital to Florence (1865-1870), when the Petraia became the favourite residence of the morganatic wife of Vittorio Emanuele, Rosa Vercellana, countess of Mirafiori (the 'Bella Rosina'), the fervour for decorating took on new fire. The choice was to be made this time from the boundless wealth of furniture, tapestries, carpets and wall coverings from the Royal palaces of all Italy,

The front of the villa from the first terrace and the pool below

after centuries come into the hands of a single monarch. The 1050 pieces that in 1865 were moved to the Petraia came from, among other places, the Villa di Marlia, the royal palaces of Lucca, Modena, Piacenza, and from the Villas of Poggio Imperiale, Poggio a Caiano and

Castello. In the general rearrangement – shown in part today on display room by room according to an *Inventory of the furnishings* drawn up in 1911 – pieces of great value were introduced, such as the Empire toilette made by Jean Baptiste Youf in 1811 or the table-desk attributed to the florentine Giovanni Socci, gems of ebony work made in Lucca for Elisa Baciocchi. The decoration of the ceilings, in white and gilded stucco or painted in *grisaille*, the rebuilding of the staircase and the installation of the warm air heating-system – a singular example of 'archeo-installation' – were directed by the Royal architects Fabio Nuti and Giusep-

rearranged, according to the designs of Ferdinando Lasinio, and given birdcages (no longer existing) and a pavilion was erected to serve as belvedere. Donated in 1919 to the Italian state, and by that to the Opera Nazionale Combattenti, the Petraia has also suffered, like Castel-

pe Giardi. Apart from the curious mixture of styles that then shaped the interior of the villa, the strongest mark made by the Savoys occurred in 1872 with the marriage of the son of Vittorio Emanuele and Rosina, Emanuele of Mirafiori. The courtyard was transformed into a feasting hall by means of a an up-to-date glass and cast-iron roof, and the the Piano della Figurina

lo and Poggio a Caiano, from long years of abandonment, aggravated by removal and the selling both of furnishings and of land. But here, too, from the sixties onwards, and even more after 1984, the year in which the Museo Nazionale was set up, the slow and difficult recovery of the villa began. Particularly in recent years, after the refurbishing of the structure, restoration and arrangement in the various rooms of paintings, furniture, porcelain, works in alabaster, carpets, till then stored, have been going on in parallel and enriching the villa as museum. Giambologna's

A detail of the Il Volterrano's fresco painted under the courtyard loggia (1637-1649)

bronze, dismantled in 1980, as was the whole *Fountain of Florence* (or *Fiorenza*) a few years later, for impelling reasons of conservation, has been put on display inside the villa. Similarly, in the only rooms meant to display other than themselves, two marble *Gladiators* and the bronze sculptures from the *Fountain of Hercules and Anteus*, from the Garden of Castello, have been set up. It is planned to include the evocative underground spaces towards the end of the visit before moving directly out into the garden. In this way one will be able to view the old kitchens, as well rooms containing models of gardens made for the *Exhibition of the Italian Gar-*

*den* held in Florence in 1931, stored since at the Petraia. The replacement outside of the *Fountain of Florence* (or *Fiorenza*) with a copy, made in 1998, will be followed by the exhibition of the original in the large space of the former stables, when it has been made ready. Though much remains to be done, the results achieved at the Petraia through the seriousness of conservation already succeeds in restoring its modern historical meaning: a glimpse of post-unification Italy which, heir to a centuries-long legacy, was sometimes, as in this case, able to reconcile new middle-class demands with the lofty grandeur of a glorious past.

## VISIT ITINERARY

### INTERIOR OF THE VILLA GROUND-FLOOR

#### Vestibule and Courtyard.
Through the vestibule, left of the which there is a self-service cafeteria, one enters the courtyard, the monumental pivot of the villa. The 'grottesche' frescoes on the two longer walls, which depict the *Deeds of Goffredo of Buglion at the taking of Jerusalem* are by Cosimo Daddi (c. 1590). Under the loggias are the *Fasti Medicei* (1637-1646), the work of Il Volterrano, depicting, from left as one enters: *The meeting between pope Leo X and Francis I of France*, *The triumphal entry of Cosimo I into Siena*, *Caterina de' Medici with her children*, *Tuscany's mastery of the sea*, *Giuliano duke of Nemours and Lorenzo duke of Urbino on the Capitoline*, *Alessandro first duke of Florence* (with self-portrait of the painter), *Cosimo II receiving the victors of the venture of Bona*, *Maria de' Medici queen of France*

with her children, *Cosimo I takes his son Francesco into government, Clement VII crowns Charles V in Bologna*. The glass and cast-iron roof and the Palladian floor were installed in 1872, along with the large chandelier in amethyst crystal, to turn the courtyard into Banquet hall, on the occasion of wedding of the son of Vittorio Emanuele and of Rosa Vercellana, Emanuele of Mirafiori, to Blanche de Larderel.

**Room of the Tapestries (Red Room).** On the right of the courtyard one comes to the large Dining Room, with Flemish tapestries from the second half of the 17th century, among which *The four Ele-*ments, The four Seasons, The months of May and June*, and, left as one enters, an important hanging made by the Arazzeria Medici on a cartoon by Agostino Melissi (1655), with *Cosimo II receiving the homage of the Senate*; as for the furniture, there are chairs and benches in Directoire style, neo-classic consoles and sofas, a eighteenth-century grandfather-clock and some 19th century clocks. The two porcelain vases on the console on the long side, decorated with *grisaille* cameos, were made by Doccia manufactory (c. 1820).

**Music Room.** The elegant hanging, in cut velvet of French manufacture, from c. 1830, comes from

The courtyard, with the 19th century covering; the frescoes under the loggia are by Il Volterrano (1637-1649), those on the counter-façade are by Cosimo Daddi

23

Lucca; the chairs and the sofas, from the late 18th century, from the Villa of Marlia; the piano-harmonium is the work of Achille Fummo di Napoli (1868); the gilt bronze clock, by Lepaute, Paris, dated 1770, comes from the royal palace of Modena.

*A detail of the frescoes of the New Chapel*

**The King's Study.** The hanging in cramoisy chiselled velvet on a gold-laminated backing, of mid 19th-century French manufacture, comes from Modena; the inlaid desk and the drum stools in Empire style, the two mirrors in carved and gilded wood and the centre table with its top of Portovenere marble, on which stand a bronze model in bronze of Trajan's Column, are admirable. The fire-screen, from Lucca, where it was made at the end of the 18th century by engravers of French taste, is laudable. Com-

ing out into the courtyard, on the right, one enters the **New Chapel**. So called to distinguish it from the Old Chapel on the first floor; the larger room, adapted as a chapel at the end of the 18th century, was originally the bedroom of the devout Cosimo III, with frescoes on the theme of the Sacred by Pier Dandini and by the painter Rinaldo Botti (c. 1696). Above the altar there is a *Holy Family*, a copy of an Andrea del Sarto.

## FIRST FLOOR

**Corridor.** Redisplayed hers, following the placing recorded in the Inventory of 1911, are numerous Chinese watercolours showing scenes with the typical subjects of the working of rice, silk, porcelain and tea, as well as a *View of the port of Canton*, painted in gouache on a silk scroll (c. 1780-1785).

**Study.** The room is decorated with French wallpaper and mid nineteenth-century mahogany furniture, on the desk is a burnished bronze lamp of French production, made from a design by Percier and Fontaine; the clocks in alabaster are from the early 19th century; the silk flower arrangement, like all the other at the Petraia, is inspired by the flowers depicted in nineteenth-century paintings.

**Empire Room.** With wall paintings dating from the Napoleonic period, divan, chairs and an elegant carpet, all from the first half of the 18th century; the two porcelain under-vases, from Marlia, decorated with *Views of Rome* in *grisaille*, are of Doccia manufacture (c. 1815-1820). The top of centre table in Empire style is in *scagliola* painted with a landscape.

**Blue Room.** The armchairs and the sofas, the hanging in blue silk with white flowers are of Lyons manufacture, the curtains, the curtain rods, the carved frames around the hanging, are all neo-rococo taste dating from the mid 19th century, and come from the Royal

**Bedroom of 'Bella Rosina'.** The hanging in sky-blue silk, of French manufacture, was bought in Florence in 1865; the bed with baldachin, from the early 19th century, comes from the Villa di Castello; among the furniture, the chest and the two cupboards in

The King's Study

palace of Modena. The porcelain is 19th century.

Through the **West Loggia** one reaches the **Studiolo di Fiorenza**. Since 1987 Giambologna's famous bronze *Florence* (or *Fiorenza*; 1570-1572), the top-piece of the marble fountain of the same name designed by Niccolò Tribolo for the Giardino di Castello (1538-1547), moved to the Piano della Figurina of Villa Petraia in 1788, has been on display here. On the opposite side of the Loggia is a small information room displaying, among other things, the design by Ferdinando Lasinio for the rearrangement of the Piano della Figurina (1872).

Left, a close-up from the Il Volterrano's frescoes under the loggia

*pendant*, the Empire cabinet, the chairs and sofa are from the first half of the 19th century; the valuable *toilette* in olive root with gild-

25

ed bronzes, the work of Jean Baptiste Gilles Youf and dated 1811, comes from Marlia; on the sofa, in a frame of neo-rococo taste, is a *Madonna with Child* modelled in wax.

One crosses the **Dressing Room**, decorated with 19th century pastels attributed to Giovanna Fratellini, with a *toilette* and an Empire 'Psyche' mirror, chairs decorated with mother-of-pearl inlays and round table with fire-marble top coming from Marlia; the **Yellow Drawing-room**, once the **King's Bedroom**, with Empire chest, chairs in *Rétour d'Egypte* style, taken from drawings by Lorenzo Nottolini, desk in Empire style attributed to the ebony artist Giovanni Socci, and hanging in silk *amuer* from Poggio a Caiano; a **Drawing-room** with fine late 18th century consoles, like the sofa and the chairs in white and gilded lacquered wood, and with 17th century tapestry door bearing the Medici arms. One passes then to the **Green Drawing-room**. The two paintings by Matteo Rosselli, *Angelica and Medoro* (1624) and *Tancredi tended by Erminia and Vafrino* (1624), were commissioned by cardinal Carlo de' Medici for the Casino di San Marco; the console and the French clock by Deverberie are from the early 19th century.

**Red Drawing-room**. The portraits are *Claudia de' Medici* by Justus Sustermans and *Henrietta of England duchess of Orléans* by Henry and Charles Beaubrun; the painting with *Bacchanal* is by Ignazio Hughford. The side table, with the elaborate neo-rococo carving, from the mid 19th century, comes from Modena.

**Old Chapel**. The wall decoration, with depictions of *Saints* and *Episodes from the life of Christ and the Saints* is the work of Bernar-

Above, the Dressing Room
Below, the Game Room

dino Poccetti, that of the ceiling, with the *Glory of the Holy Spirit among Angels and the Elect*, is attributed to Cosimo Daddi (1589-94); over the altar is a copy of Raphael's *Madonna of the Impannata*.

**Game Room**. The room was furnished by the Lorraine between 1853 and 1861 with the sofas, the small armchairs, the chairs and small chairs, the sultana and the *vis-à-vis*, upholstered in Indian chintz, and the three mahogany consoles of Florentine manufacture. A billiard table, the two branched lamps and the fine table from the early 19th century, holding many games, among them roulette, draughts and the *trottola americana*, were added to the furniture after 1865. The fine alabaster is from the first half of the 19th century. The seventeenth-century paintings are (from left to right): *Semiramis* by Matteo Rosselli, *Artemisia* by Francesco Curradi, *Erminia among the shepherds* by Francesco Curradi (1633), *Amphion on the dolphin*, by Domenico Cresti known as Il Passignano, *Rinaldo in the garden of Armida* by Domenico Frilli Croci (1624), *Olindo and Sofronia freed by Clorinda* by Francesco Rustici (before 1624).

**East Loggia**. Among the finest pieces of furniture in the villa are the two table-tops in wood inlaid with plant and animal motifs attributed to Leonardo Van Der Vinne (1686), highpoints of Baroque ebony work.

**Dining Room**. The modest tone of the furnishings of this room, 'ordinary' mid 19th century, is raised by the important carpet, a rare example of Florentine manufacture, signed and dated 1806 by Girolamo Podestà; among the 17th and 18th century paintings are the *Portraits of Carlo II of Lorraine* and of *Maria*

*Maddalena de' Medici*. One descends into the courtyard, to move into the **Room of Hercules and Anteus**. So called after the recent showing of the famous bronze by Bartolomeo Ammannati portraying *Hercules raising Anteus* (1559-1560), moved in 1978 for reasons of conservation

from the *Fountain of Hercules and Anteus* in the Giardino di Castello, on display here till the fountain is re-assembled in the villa from which it came; the adjoining room on the left (under preparation in 2003) holds other pieces of the same fountain, among which, through a original simulation of the basin they

The *Venus-Florence* (or *Fiorenza*) by Giambologna, inside the 'Studiolo di Fiorenza'

27

bestrode, four bronze putti, three by Pierino da Vinci and one by Niccolò Tribolo.

Through two rooms displaying some Chinese watercolours from the series bought by Pietro Leopoldo around 1785, and one of the garden models made for the *Exhibition of the* of an ancient sculpture (head, torso and right thigh), thought to have come from a copy of the famous Apoxymenos by Lysippus. Among the paintings, two *Landscapes with wayfarers* by Crescenzio Onofri with figures by Alessandro Magnasco (c. 1708).

The Belvedere

*Italian Garden* held in Florence in 1931, one comes to the **Room of the Gladiators**. Since 1998 the room holds the two sculptures of *Gladiators* made by Domenico Pieratti after 1635, moved for reasons of conservation from the Giardino di Castello and replaced there by two casts.

The sculptures were made for the amphitheatre in the Boboli Gardens, from which they were taken almost immediately to the Uffizi, to be moved then to Castello in 1780. While the one with the shield, finished in 1647, is by Pieratti, the other was made to fill out the fragment

## BASEMENTS

One goes down in the basement to visit the old kitchens (under restoration in 2003), and the rooms that house the models of gardens made for the *Exhibition of the Italian Garden* held in Florence in 1931, stored at Villa della Petraia.

## GARDEN AND PARK

Coming out from villa, on the right is the **West Level**, rearranged in the time of the Savoys with cedars; downhill lie the remains of the 'lime

of Vittorio Emanuele', used as tree-house by the royals. Towards the east is the **Piano della Figuri-na**. So called from the famous sculpture of Venus-Florence by Giambologna that topped the fountain of the same name, the work of Niccolò Tribolo and Pierino from Vinci (1538-1547), moved here in 1788 from Villa di Castello; the fountain is a cast of the original. In the south-east corner stand the pavilion of the **Belvedere**. Described in the old Inventories as *Reposoir*, because it functioned as a resting-place during walks in the park, it was built in 1872 as part of the re-modelling of the Piano della Figu-rina designed by the architect Fer-dinando Lasinio. It has been refur-nished with the original furniture and with curtaining based on that mentioned in the Inventory of 1911, which has disappeared. Through the gate closing the wall garden

one visits the Romantic **Park** to the north of the villa, measuring about 50 acres, conceived with a landscaper's taste by Joseph Fri-etsch in 1829. Its paths wind around two ponds and to a fine wood of evergreens and conifers. In virtue of the needs it serve, especially as stopover for migrating birds, since 2003 the park contains a wildlife reserve managed by the LIPU (Ital-ian League for the Protection of Birds), the first of the kind in Italy. One re-enters the walled Garden to descend to the **Nursery level**, where there is a garden done in nineteenth-century taste on the east and, on the other side, a gar-den of bulbous plants in front of the Warm Room.

The **parterres**, laid out at the begin-ning of the 19th century, are plant-ed with dwarf fruit trees, harking back to a genre typical of the six-teenth-century garden.

The Piano della Figurina

# Villa di Castello

The Villa di Castello – also called 'L'Olmo' (the Elm), or 'Il vivaio' (the Nursery) – standing along the line of a Roman aqueduct from the cisterns (*castellum*) of which the place gets its name, is one of the oldest Medici properties. An earlier fortified building, already existing in 1427, belonging among others to the Della Stufa family, was sold by them in 1477 to Lorenzo and Giovanni di Pierfrancesco de' Medici, of the cadet branch of the family, who undertook the rebuilding. The new construction, with courtyard, ground-floor room with loggia, kitchens and stables, passed then in inheritance to the war-leader Giovanni dalle Bande Nere, husband of Maria Salviati and father of Cosimo de' Medici, who spent his childhood there.

## HOW TO GET THERE

Between Sesto Fiorentino and Careggi, near Quinto.
Home to the Accademia della Crusca.
*Address* via di Castello 47,
Castello (Florence).
*Bus* 2, 28
*Tel* +39 055 454791
*Opening times* (tickets sale stops 1 1/2 h before closing time) 8:15-17 (Nov thru Feb); 8:15-18 (March); 8:15-19 (Apr, May, Sep, Oct); 8:15-20 (Jun-Aug).
Closed the second and third Monday of the month.
*Entry* € 2.00 (full); € 1.00 (reduced).
The visit is only to the park of villa.
The ticket also covers a visit to Villa della Petraia if made on the same day.
Guided tour inside the 'Grotto of the Animals' and 'Ortaccio'.

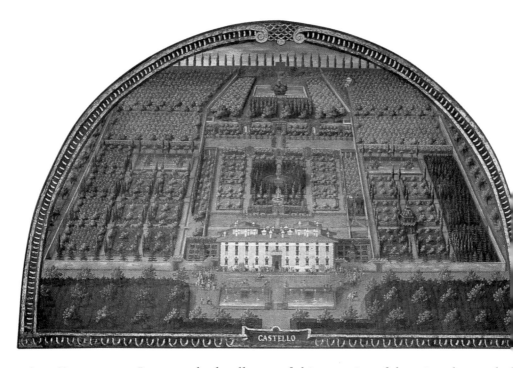

Justus Utens,
*Villa di Castello,*
1599-1602;
Florence, Museo
storico topografico
'Firenze com'era'

It was undoubtedly out of this personal affection that the young Cosimo, after his lightning rise in the few months between January and July 1537, from Duke of Florence and then victor over the republican rebels at Montemurlo, "having come through as he did – so Vasari narrates – the trials he had in the first year of his princeship...began to take some leisure, and particularly to frequent the villa di Castello". With the aid of the hydraulic engineer Piero da San Casciano, of advisers among whom Benedetto Varchi, but especially the sculptor and architect Niccolò Tribolo, a keen interpreter of Michelangelo's Mannerism and true 'soul' of the project, in a few years Cosimo I gave shape in his favourite residence to a brilliant idea of political propaganda whereby the garden became, in the magnificence of its fountains and sculptures, an allegory of the affir-

mation of the princedom and of its territorial ambitions. That is why the Castello garden, entirely conceived in 1538 according to a project that Vasari describes down to the smallest detail, though never quite finished, was to stand as the model for a new culture of the garden as display of personal and dynastic power, the unignorable example for the great Medici gardens that were soon to follow, but also, more generally, for the Italian and European gardens of the Renaissance. The ambitious design of Cosimo and his artists transformed the hilly nature of the place into a work of architecture: through the large-scale earth-moving and the canalisation of the waters from the nearby springs of the Castellina and the Petraia, the new arrangement took shape up the slope as two main terraces, with the geometrical garden on the lower and the 'wilderness' on the upper. The

'descending' iconography from the hill towards the villa reflects the geographical conformation of Tuscany and the course of the two rivers that bathe Florence: the bronze sculpture by Bartolomeo Ammannati depicting *The Apennines* (1563), which dominates the large pond in the 'wild' garden, is conceptually linked to the two 'rustic' fountains called *Monti Senario* and *Falterona* set in the retaining wall below, the waters from which flow down in their turn to the representations of the respective rivers, the *Mugnone with Fiesole* and the *Arno*, set along the transverse wall that divided the lower garden in two. Medici control of Florence and Tuscany were instead celebrated along the central axis in 'ascendant' iconography beginning from the villa: the *Fountain of Hercules and Anteus*, alluding to Cosimo's victory over the republican exiles, sculpted by Tribolo with the help of Pierino da Vinci

and completed by Bartolomeo Ammannati with the bronze group on the summit, higher up, in the centre of a thick maze of greenery, the *Fountain of Florence* (or *Fiorenza*) – the work of Tribolo and of Pierino crowned by the famous bronze by Giambologna – a metaphor, through the allegory of Venus-Florence who rules the Gardens of the Hesperides, of the triumph of Florence over the nascent Grand-duchy; and behind, dug into the embankment of the wild garden, the 'Grotto of the Animals', or 'of the Flood'. This grotto, unique of its kind and almost wholly intact, 'flooded' by streams of water springing from the ceiling and floor and splashing into three great marble basins, clad with limestone concretions studded with mosaics and shells, enlivened by phantasmagorical figures in polychrome marble and bronze of creature of water, land and air, among which stands out the mag-

The extended main front of the villa

33

ical unicorn, a symbol of purity, was designed to allude, through the symbolism expressed by a statue of *Orpheus with the lyre* originally set in the middle of the grotto, to Cosimo's thaumaturgical pacification of the living universe. The sculptures that were to stand along the side walls of the geometrical garden referred to the seasons of the year, to the virtues of the Medici house and to the benefits it brought to Florence.

The programme celebrating the new Medici springtime, made tangible in the vast outdoor space thanks also to the exuberant plant-life and the spectacular play of water – the six cubit (more than three metres) jet that rose from the mouth of Anteus was one of the marvels – was matched inside the villa by two paintings by Botticelli depicting *Spring* and the *Birth of Venus*, moved there by Cosimo before 1550, and in the cycle of paintings done by Pontormo in a ground-floor loggia between 1538 and 1543, depicting the *Return of the Golden Age*. Below the imposing dwelling, beyond the two nurseries in the outer court, a picturesque avenue shaded by a 'portico' of mulberry trees, flanked all along by two canal with fish and prawns, was to reach as far as the Arno.

After Tribolo's death in 1550 the work went on under Davide Fortini and then Vasari, scrupulously following the former's designs over two decades. Neither the garden nor the planned doubling of the villa was ever achieved by Cosimo, distracted in the meantime by new projects for the ducal apartments in Palazzo Vecchio and above all for the Reggia di Pitti, bought in 1549.

Only between 1588 and 1595, having been inherited by Ferdinando I, the villa was completed by Buontalenti in its present form with the enlargement on the east side, the rearrangement of the two facades, the new entrance on the south side. The lunette painted by Just Utens at the end of the century shows it as it was then, with a tournament taking place in the meadow in front, under the eyes of a colourful crowd. The perspective of the villa and garden, in actuality quite askew, has been corrected by Utens who aligned them with perfect symmetry. The careful depiction of the garden gives, along with Vasari's description, fundamental evidence of how it must have looked at the period of its greatest splendour when it received the enthusiastic praise of travellers such as Michel de Montaigne (who visited it on two occasions, in 1580 and 1581) and Joseph Furttenbach, or of botanists like Pierre Belon.

The property later passed through the hands of many members of the Medici house without undergoing any important changes. After for some time housing Maria Maddalena of Austria, on her coming to Florence for her wedding to Cosimo II, Cristina of Lorraine, who died there in 1636, and the cultivated Don Lorenzo – whose refined patronage is witnessed by the fine fresco by Il Volterrano of *Wake and Sleep* (c. 1640) – the villa was to go through a period of high-spirited splendour thanks to the ebullient cardinal Giovan Carlo, who died there 1663 after filling it with banquets and lavish festivities but not with any other significant 'legacies' (except a fresco with his coat-of-arms visible in the woodshed at the top the park). Cosimo III's learned curiosity – he frequently visited the vineyards, and also stayed in neighbouring Topaia – was instead to endow the garden with one of its most precious botanical rarities, to go along with the prickly pears cactus already planted in the sixteenth-century garden: the Indian jasmine known as 'mugherino', given to the Grand-duke by the King of Portugal in 1688, was to be cultivated from then on at Castello. In the cold months it is taken inside into a purpose-built greenhouse, the 'Stufa dei [Stove of the] mugherini', in the eastern secret garden. When the Medici died out, large restructuring works were undertaken by the House of Lorraine in their usual style, functional rather than for display. In that period, apart from the considerably attention given to enlarging and looking after the fine collection of citrus fruit (with the construction of the two Lemon Houses) and the laying-out of the English garden, linked by a carriageway to that of Villa della Petraia, the sculptures and garden decorations, the product of an artistic and political climate by then remote and incomprehensible to a culture shaped by the crystalline reason of the Enlightenment, were neglected. In the utilitarian management of the new grand-dukes nurseries were buried, Tribolo's 'rustic' fountains dismantled, the wall at the bottom of the garden rebuilt in neo-classic style, the rockery replaced, the water cut off in the grotto, the marvellous correlation between the two central fountains broken for ever, the woody maze destroyed and the *Fountain of Hercules and Anteus* shifted to the middle of the garden in place of the *Fountain of Florence* (or *Fiorenza*) moved in 1788 to Villa della Petraia. Nor did the insertion of classical busts or the two gladiators in the niches of the far

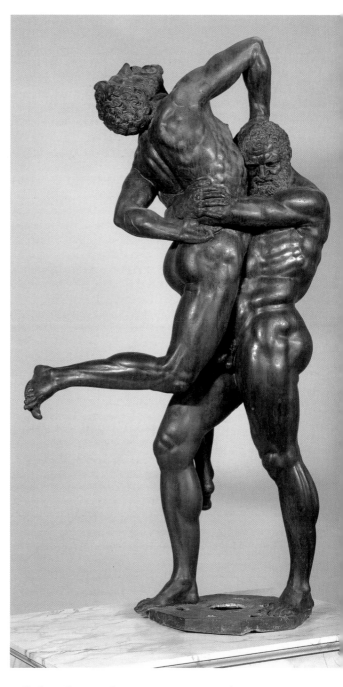

wall, the reflection of an antiquarian collectionism, knowledgeable but removed from the substantial classicism of the sixteenth-century design, redeem the losses.

Bartolomeo Ammannati *Hercules and Anteus*, whose original is at La Petraia

35

After that, with the notable addition of decorative painting in neoclassic style done in the Napoleonic period, progressive abandonment and lack of maintenance marked the fate of the complex which, neglected also by the House of Savoy, who preferred the nearby Petraia, underwent rapid decline. Donated in 1919 to the Italian State, stripped of its furnishings, given over to a variety of purposes (dwellings for the gardeners, elementary schools, military hospital), it had to wait until the sixties for an essentially architectonic restoration – that however got rid of a great deal of its 18-19th century decoration – and to be turned into the home of the respected Accademia della Crusca, the body that occupies it today.

As for the garden, open since then to the public, it was designated national museum in 1984, along with the neighbouring Villa della Petraia. Thus work was undertaken on the woods, the park, the secret garden of the Grand-duke – with the inclusion of aromatic and medicinal herbs – restoration done on the Lemon Houses, the sculptures, the interior of 'Grotto of the Animals' (where the original hydraulic system with the famous jets of water is now under repair). Conservation work is also under way on the fountains, seriously damaged by years of exposure in the open, and that, here as at Petraia, are masterpieces of sixteenth-century Florentine sculpture. In particular the *Fountain of Hercules and Anteus,* the easily dismantled parts of which have been in storage for over twenty years, has been entirely taken apart for restoration, and is to be replaced outside by a cast and be re-erected in the court of the villa, the only fitting place for Tri-

A view
of the central part
of the garden.
The *Fountain
of Hercules and
Anteus* is presently
dismantled
for restoration

bolo's imposing device. A 'suspended' cover is to be built for it, using contemporary forms and materials, in line with what is now a worldwide tendency to recuperate spaces (one thinks of the covered courtyards of the Palais du Louvre in Paris or of the British Museum in London), something successfully done by the Savoys

in 1872 when they had the court-yard of Villa della Petraia covered. The recently designed project of improvement of the Garden of Castello as museum includes the creation of a Visitors' Centre with information rooms and self-service cafeteria in the small building in front of the entry and the floodlighting of the garden at night,

to create an unusual and evocative *plein air* alternative to the traditional Florence museums.

## VISIT ITINERARY

From the gate one enters the geometrical garden along the side of the villa. In front, a small build-

Here and at the
following page,
the 'Grotto of the
Animals'

ing holds a visitors' centre, with information rooms and a buffet (in progress). One continues left to reach the central axis of the **Lower Garden**.

One goes up to the *Fountain of Hercules and Anteus*, a cast (to be made in 2003) of the original, dismantled in stages between 1980 and 1997, because of its advance state of decay. The Fountain was conceived and sculpted by Niccolò Tribolo, with the collaboration of Pierino da Vinci, between 1538 and 1548; the bronze group on the top, portraying *Hercules and Anteus*, is by Bartolomeo Ammannati (1559-1560). The classical

sculptures that surround the basin, like the busts on the buttresses of the transverse wall that divides the Lower Garden in two, assembled in the 18th century from pieces that did then belong together, were set in the garden under the House of Lorraine, during the restructuring of 1785-1788.

One continues through the divisions of the garden, with dwarf fruit-trees within box hedges, going up of the **Garden of Citrus Fruits**. So called since the 16th century, it still holds the largest and oldest plants of the famous Castello collection of citrus fruits (about 500 exemplars in pots, apart from those

espaliered ones and the shrubs). Among them, is also the *bizzarria*, got by grafting. The stamping ground immediately at the top of the steps is decorated with polychrome pebbles, and has jets of water spraying from the ground. **Grotto of the Animals**. The grotto, also called **'of the Flood'** with its marvellous jets of water was begun by Niccolò Tribolo after 1538 and completed by Giorgio Vasari about 40 years later. The marble basin on the left is attributed to Tribolo himself; the one on the right is instead from his workshop. The bronze birds done by Bartolomeo Ammannati and Giambologna, originally attached to the roof or perched on the walls, are now on show at the Bargello Museum. The sculptures of animals in polychrome stone and marble, mimicking the natural colours of the animals, are attributed to Antonio Lorenzi, Tribolo's collaborator. The central niche contains the magical unicorn, symbol of purity, alluding to Cosimo I work of cleansing the state. The grotto originally held a representation of Orpheus, mentioned by early travellers, removed at an unknown date. The myth of Orpheus who with the music of his lyre tames and spellbinds the wild

The 'Ortaccio' and the 'Stufa dei mugherini'

beasts and animals of the creation translated Cosimo's pacification of Tuscany after his rise to power into an allegory.

The wall in which the grotto opens has two niches with basins and sculptures of **Gladiators** (casts, the originals are on show in Villa della Petraia), the work of Domenico Pieratti (after 1635), originally in the Boboli Garden, then in the Uffizi, and from 1780 at Castello. The left-hand one was made by replacing pieces of an ancient fragmentary sculpture, probably a copy of the famous *Apoxyómenos* by Lysippus. At the corner of the garden of citrus fruit stand the two large lemon houses (before 1785).

Along the wall on the east side there is door leading to the so-called '**Ortaccio**'. On the left of the walled garden stands a shapely building from the second half of the 18th century, called the '**Stufa dei mugherini**', from the name of the famous double jasmine

from Goa known as the 'Mugheri-no of the Grand-duke of Tuscany', introduced to Florence by Cosimo III in 1688. In the garden, planted with aromatic and medicinal herbs, is a sculpture representing *Autumn* (under restoration in 2003), belonging perhaps to the series of the *Four Seasons* mentioned by Vasari as standing in the sixteenth-century garden. Two flights of steps at the corners of the embankment wall lead up to the **Upper Garden**. In the middle of the 'wilderness' is the large basin-fishpond called the ***Apennines***, from bronze sculpture by Bartolomeo Ammannati (1563-1565) occupying the rock set in the middles of the water. An umbrella-shaped jet of water rises from its peak. The basin acts as reservoir for the hydraulic system of the lower garden. One leaves the garden through the English park, laid out by the House of Lorraine in the third decade of the 19th century.

The statue of the *Apennines*, by Bartolomeo Ammannati

41

# Villa di Poggio a Caiano

The building of the Villa Medici of Poggio a Caiano began in 1474 with the acquisition of land in the area between Poggio a Caiano, Bonistallo, Castelnuovo and Tavola by Lorenzo the Magnificent. Conceived from the start within a more ample project, following the model handed down from classical antiquity, it was to have farms and pasture land connected to it that would provide the villa, a place of contemplative ease and display of dynastic power, with income. Its designing came some years after the setting up of the 'Cascine' farm, stretching along the plain on the other side of the river Ombrone, immediately below the site chosen for the building. Once the area had been made safe by large-scale embanking of the river, the 'Cascine', the main building of which – a square construction surrounded by a ditch, with bastions at the corners and large internal courtyard – went up in 1477, stirred the admiration of the circle of humanists gravitating round Lorenzo (Michele

## HOW TO GET THERE

In the centre of Poggio a Caiano.
*Address* piazza dei Medici 12, Poggio a Caiano (Prato).
*Tel* + 39 55 877012
*Opening times* (tickets sale stops 1 1/2 h before closing time) 8:15-17 (Nov thru Feb); 8:15-18 (March); 8:15-17 (Apr, May, Sep, Oct); 8:15-20 (Jun-Aug). Closed the second and third Monday of the month.
*Entry* € 2.00 (full); € 1.00 (reduced).
Guided tour inside.

Verino was to devote a poem to it), because of the efficiency of the irrigation canal, its wealth of orchards, mulberry trees and meadows, its stockbreeding and production of milk and cheese.

With the land Lorenzo had also bought from Giovanni Rucellai a fortified building, set on a hill over

the Ombrone, described in 1480 as "a building that was in ruins at Poggio a Caiano, called the Ambra" (Lorenzo was to devote to the Ambra, understood as the site of the villa, a celebrated little poem). Around 1485, when the first stage of the revolutionary and humanist project had been completed with the finishing of the 'Cascine', Lorenzo turned to a trusted architect, Giuliano da Sangallo, to replace the old fortified building with a new construction, to be erected on its foundations.

Trained in the new architecture of Brunelleschi and fortified by first-hand study of archaeologi-

The main front of the villa with the 18th century stairways

43

cal remains during his long stay in Rome (1465-1471), Sangallo built, "according to the whim" and with the advice of Lorenzo, a passionate student of architecture, the building that was to be-resulting from the mathematical and geometrical calculation of the forms was translated into an admirable harmony of proportions. The traditional inner courtyard disappeared to make way for an

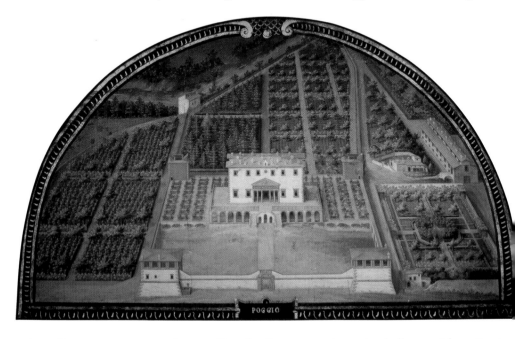

Justus Utens, *Villa di Poggio a Caiano*, 1599-1602; Florence, Museo storico topografico 'Firenze com'era'

come the paradigm for the country villa in the Humanist period. The result was totally innovative: no longer the villa-fort on the Michelozzo model, but a new typology of villa which, set on a natural hill, raised further by an underground structure meant for the various services and by a tall porticoed basement on the ground-floor – the *basis villae* of Roman architecture – rose with the white coating outlined by the grey of the prospects achieving a new relationship with the surrounding space which it dominated and contemplated at the same time. The villa extended towards the lands controlled by the Prince by means of the terrace that surrounded it on every side, allowing an all-round and endless view. The symmetry

imposing hall, meant from it original conception to magnify and exalt the glories of the family. The loggia, with Ionic columns and frontal bearing the Medici coat of arms, is encapsulated within the main facade, solemn as the pronaos of an ancient temple. An analogous attitude towards the classic, understood as ideological and cultural reference as well as stylistic and formal, shaped the few essays in decoration undertaken in Lorenzo's time: the frieze in glazed terracotta of the architrave of the pronaos, that illustrated through a complex neo-Platonic programme the possible options for the soul and the cyclic rhythm of the life of the fields, and, within the same loggia, the barrel-vaulting decorated with stucco and the

unfinished fresco by Filippino Lippi depicting *The sacrifice of Laocoon*. Lorenzo's ambitious project, extending to the distribution of the main interior rooms, was interrupted by his death in 1492, by which time only a third of the villa had been built, and only the front part finished. Political events, due to fatal turns of fortune – fortune that, as we are reminded by the motto of Giuliano duke of Nemours "glovis", read backwards, "si volg[e]", it turns – were to prevent his son Piero, driven from Florence in 1494 by the coming of the republic, from bringing it to completion.

It was not until 1512, with the return of Lorenzo duke of Urbino from exile, and above all until 1513, with the triumphant rise to the papal throne of the Magnificent's son, Giovanni, under the name of Leo X, that the work regained its full rhythm. The hall, with barrel-vaulting in stucco decorated with the Medici coat of arms and emblem – the ring of diamonds with plumes, the burning bough, the yoke – and the engagement of such artists as Pontormo, Andrea del Sarto and Franciabigio for the creation of the cycle of eulogistic paintings wanted by the Pope and conceived by the historian Paolo Giovio, date from this period.

With the death of Leo X in 1521 the work stopped for the second time. Cosimo I, driven by the ambition to celebrate in allegorical fashion his own role rather than that of an ancestor, and one from an indirect branch into the bargain, spent most of his efforts on the Vil-

The façade, with gable and ornamental frieze

la di Castello, the Uffizi and Palazzo Pitti, neglecting, at Poggio a Caiano, to complete the 'Leo X Room', turning instead to the construction, on a design of Niccolò Tribolo, of the grandiose enclosure with corner bulwarks of the Italian garden on the side towards Florence and of the stables, well documented by Utens in the lunette painted in 1599 for the Villa di Artimino. As for the interior decorations, following his passion for hunting, which was to find its vent in the grandiose reserve of 'Barco Reale' at Monte Albano, of which the villa was the main point of reference, he got the 'Arazzeria' Medici, which he founded, to make a extraordinary series of tapestries on cartoons by Stradano and Allori, depicting the various types of hunting, four for each of the twenty main rooms of the villa (stored today in the Florentine museums).

After him Francesco I – who inherited by the wish of Cosimo, the latter having assigned the villa in 1568 to the firstborn sons of the family – was to take up the project of decorating the *salone* using Vincenzo Borghini, getting the missing scenes provided and those done by Alessandro Allori (1578-1582) modified. Scenes and magniloquent representations were produced, evocative of the luxury of the grand-ducal court of his time rather than of the illustrious history of his ancestor Lorenzo. To Francesco's frequent stays in the villa and to those of his Venetian mistress, later wife, the ground-floor suite came to be called the apartment 'of Bianca Cappello'. It was there on, 19 October 1587, that the destiny of both Francesco and Bianca was settled, probably a matter of natural causes, though legend tells it was brought about by the cunning and poison of his

brother cardinal Ferdinando, who was to succeed him as Grand-duke. Lived in regularly in the time of Cosimo III, who for some years confined there in 'golden' but forced isolation his rebellious and capricious bride, Marguerite Louise d'Orléans, before her final return to France in 1675, the villa was endowed with a theatre on the ground-floor for the amusement of the Grand-duchess and her retinue of more than a hundred and fifty people. The passion for the theatre, endowed in the meantime with a fine organ dated 1703, still to be seen there, was shared by the royal couple's son, Grand Prince Ferdinando, during his frequent stays at Poggio in the company of musicians and actors. Thus the flair and expertise of the refined cognoscente was to add to the existing collections such rooms as the 'Bedroom of Venetian paintings', decorated with a lost fresco by Sebastiano Ricci, or the 'Cabinet of Minute works', destined to hold a plethora of paintings by the most celebrated painters, as many as one hundred and seventy-four in a single room, all strictly of tiny dimensions. Though these works were removed after 1773 to the Galleries in Florence, there is still evidence in the present 'Dining Room' of the artistic taste of the Grand Prince, the fresco by Anton Domenico Gabbiani, showing the *Apotheosis of Cosimo the Elder*.

When Gian Gastone de' Medici died without heirs in 1737 and the Lorraine Hapsburgs came in, the 'Imperial and Royal Villa of Poggio a Caiano' – the title assumed after 1745 when Francesco Stefano was elected emperor – became an object of attention and of restoration, directed by the architects Giuseppe and Giovan Battista Ruggeri. Their task was mainly maintenance except for the refurbishing of the theatre on the ground-floor and the creation of the showcase for the clock on top of the facade.

The use of the country dwelling chiefly as a place for relaxation which the Baroque period replac-

swing, a 'donkey roundabout' and a 'horse roundabout', still preserved in a storeroom.

The occupation of the city by French troops on 25 March 1799, with the exiling of the Lorraine that followed, brusquely and for ever interrupted the substantial-

ed its use a base for autumn hunting, was to culminate under the new grand-duke Ferdinando III, in line with the taste for amusement of an epoch by then close to its end, in the singular amusement park set up by Ruggeri on the front meadow, which included a 'flying spinning-wheel', a

ly continuous process of management and 'embellishment' that had characterised the use of the villa. The new demand for a return to the classic as model for a ordered and rational expression of power, first republican and then imperial, represented in Florence by Marie Louise de Bour-

The left stairway to the villa

bon, queen of Etruria from 1803 to 1807, and by Elisa Baciocchi, grand-duchess of Tuscany from 1809 to 1814, was as the basis of the radical renewal in line with neo-classic taste undertaken at

concentrated their interest on the garden with the construction of the great lemon house and the redesigning of the park in the English fashion, came the last historical stage in modification to San-

A perspective with the porticoed ground floor

that time. It is expressed in the new and monumental staircases built by Pasquale Poccianti on the facade and inside at the expense of the originals, as is the fresco decoration, the work of various artists among whom Luigi Catani from Prato stands out, of as many as seventeen rooms of the villa.

After the Restoration, and the tranquillity of the second Lorraine period (1814-1859), when they

gallo's building, consequent on the unification of Italy (1861) and the transfer of the capital from Turin to Florence (1865-70).

It was in this period that the villa, visited from time to time by Vittorio Emanuele II and his morganatic wife Rosa Vercellana (the 'Bella Rosina'), was entirely 'renovated' according to the taste of the new rulers. If on the one hand the mural decorations of some rooms, such as 'the billiard' or 'dining' room or and the ground-floor, were changed under the direction of the architect Antonio Sailer, on the other the entire *mobilier* was renewed by importing furniture from the Royal palaces of the whole of Italy, from Turin, Parma, Modena, Lucca and Bologna, now become the property of the new single kingdom.

Donated to the state, like many other Crown properties, in 1919, its function as country dwelling for the reigning family now over, the villa was to undergo a long period of decay, removal and irreversible changes, among which the stripping of furniture and hangings from the second floor, in the intention of restoring it to the supposed simplicity of the original project. After 1984, the year it became a national museum, the restoration of many parts of the villa, of the garden and park began again. The existence of a detailed *Inventory of the furnishings* drawn up in 1911 which 'photographed' the actual conditions in the Savoy period has made it possible, through the recuperation of furniture, paintings and objects scattered through various museums and state deposits, the detailed refurnishing of the various rooms according to the last significant historical configuration. The refurnishing is still till in progress.

Further restoration will be necessary to make visitable service areas or such unusual and fascinating features as the large seventeenth-century kitchen, the underground 'cryptoporticus', the 'Tennis Room', or to set up new display sections on the second floor; to ensure that the villa, the extraordinary museum of itself, can be enjoyed in a full mirroring of the rich and variegated history that made it alive in the long course of time.

## VISIT ITINERARY

### INTERIOR OF THE VILLA GROUND-FLOOR

**Portico and Vestibule**. Through the portico, decorated with 'grottesques' in 1865, where stand four sarcophagi from Roman times, coming from Medici antiquarian collections, one comes to the Vestibule, the murals of which go from neo-Renaissance

A detail of a stairway on the park side

49

Above, hanging
stairway in 'pietra
serena' sandstone
inside the Bianca
Cappello apartment

Below, curtain
of the theatre
with the images
of *Apollo and Minerva*

motifs to still-lifes and hunting trophies (1865), the result of the enthusiasm for the sport of Vittorio Emanuele II first king of Italy, as recorded in the two inscriptions on the side walls. The gilt bronze chandelier (1821) comes from Palazzo Pitti; the four *consoles* and stools are from the neo-classic period, while the two bench chests have the Savoy coat of arms in the centre.

**Theatre Room**. The present stage and scenery were constructed in 1772 for Pietro Leopoldo of Lorraine to replace an earlier theatre built before 1675 for the use of Marguerite Louise d'Orléans and her Court, at the time of her voluntary exile in the villa; the curtain, depicting *Apollo and Minerva*, was painted after 1809 by one of the painters of Elisa Baciocchi, sister of Napoleon and new grand-duchess of Tuscany, perhaps Luigi Catani from Prato, responsible for other paintings in the villa.

**Billiard Room**. Decorated by artists in the circle of the Ferri of Turin, painters and set-designers who came to Florence in the King's retinue in 1865, the room is occupied by two large billiard tables from the early nineteenth century; the rest of the furniture, from the middle of the same century, comes in part from ducal palace of Piacenza, and was moved to the villa in 1867.

**Apartment of Bianca Cappello**. Through a room holding two paintings, *Moses and the burning bush* and *The crossing of the Red Sea*, attributed to Paolo Veronese, one reaches the apartment where in the second half of the sixteenth century grand-duchess Bianca Cappello lodged, as a plaque on the right wall records. To the period of Francesco I's second wife belong the staircase in pietra serena and

The Billiard Room

the marble fireplace in the first room, while the next room, believed to be the 'Bedroom of Bianca', upholstered in stamped leather and with furniture in neo-sixteenth-century taste, was completely renovated 'in stile' after 1865.

## FIRST FLOOR

Up the monumental **staircase** designed by the court architect Pasquale Poccianti before 1808, after having visited the **Field Bedroom of Vittorio Emanuele**, containing fold-up furniture made by the Martinotti of Turin and bought at the National Exhibition of Florence in 1861, through the original **Entry Room** – decorated with monochrome frescoes by Luigi Catani depicting *Lorenzo the Magnificent receiving the model of the villa from Giuliano da Sangallo*, and *Angelo Poliziano crowning the bust of Homer with laurels*, allud-

ing to the period of the foundation of the villa, and holding neo-classic furniture from Modena and Lucca – one passes to the **Southwest apartments.** The various rooms set laterally to the 'Entry Room', used as apartments during the Savoy period, have been refurnished following, where possible, the arrangement recorded in the Inventory of 1911.

Worth noting, in the first room on the west side (to the right as one enters), are the paintings by Bartolomé González, with the portraits of Philip IV of Spain and Anna of Austria, and, in the next, two *consoles* in Empire style, some armchairs from the ducal palace of Parma and the large inclinable mirror of the 'Psyche' type. On the south side, after a glance at a drawing-room with furniture and objects of varying provenance (Lucca, Parma, Modena), among which an elegant Biedermeier desk, the chandelier in gilt bronze and blown glass from the mid 19th century, two Piedmontese oil paintings and three watercolours with *Alpine landscapes,* and a pair of *pots-pourris* of Parisian manufacture by Jacob Petit, all from the 19th century, one passes to the **Room of the Frieze**. The large room, the outcome of putting two rooms together, has for some years housed the famous glazed terracotta Frieze once mounted within the architrave of the pronaos of the facade, where it has been replaced by a cast. The fascinating frieze is a mystery in terms of its maker – Andrea Sansovino, Giuliano da Sangallo, Bertoldo – dating – before the death of the Magnificent (1492) or in two phases, the second after the election of Leo X (1513) – and theme depicted – the options for souls according to the

Some details
from the polychrome
terracotta frieze
once standing
on the main gable

Andrea di Cosimo
Feltrini, detail
of the decoration
of the barrel-vaulting,
with polychrome
stucco
(1519-1521),
in the 'Leo X Room'

Platonic myth or the return of the cosmic and earthly Golden Age – is, for these very reasons, an expression of the complex and initiatic cultural climate that characterised the period of Lorenzo the Magnificent, to whose *entourage* of learned and refined humanist, including, among others, Marsilio Ficino, Angelo Poliziano, Michele Verino, the genesis of the work is to be traced. In is in any case embed with an evocative and almost heartbreaking classicism.

**Leo X Room**. The veritable monumental pivot of the villa, destined from the start to display and exalt the glories of the family, left unfinished by the exiling of Piero de' Medici in 1494, was completed in its structural part was after the election to the papal throne of Giovanni, son of the Magnificent, as Leo X, for whom it is named. The emblems of Giovanni, along with those of the family, mark off the rich decoration in polychrome stucco of the grandiose barrel-vaulting, poured in concrete into obverse moulds. Of the imposing cycle of frescoes, organised as a celebration of the life of Cosimo the Elder and of Lorenzo through episodes of the history of Rome, and done in two stages (from 1513 to 1521, and from 1578 to 1582), the one that stands out for its pictorial quality and power is the lunette with *Vertumnus and Pomona* (above right), done between 1519 and 1520 by Jacopo Carucci known as Il Pontormo. It alludes through the myth of the two rustic deities and the presence of the laurels springing from the cut boughs, to the cyclical continuity of nature accompanying the resurgent Medici stock. The wall squares illustrate (from the right as one enters) *The consul Flaminius speaking to the council of the Acheans* by Alessandro Allori, *Return of Cicero from exile* by Francesco di Cristofano known as Il Franciabigio, *Syphax king of Numidia receiving Scipio* by Allori, creator also of the lunette on the left with *Hercules and Good Fortune guarding the Garden of the Hesperides*, and lastly, *The tribute to Caesar* by Andrea del Sarto.

**Dining Room**. The fresco in the centre of the ceiling, by Anton Domenico Gabbiani, showing the *Apotheosis of Cosimo the Elder*, was originally surrounded by rich stucco decoration, replaced in 1865 by the present decoration, more suited to the taste of the Savoys,

Above,
the lunette with
*Vertumnus
and Pomona*
by Pontormo
(c. 1519-1520)
in the 'Leo X Room'

as is the mantel-piece mirror in neo-Renaissance style; the two pieces of furniture at the sides of the entry wall, neo-Baroque taste, date from the mid 19th century and come from Parma.

**Apartment of Vittorio Emanuele.** This part of the villa takes its name from the first king of Italy. It consists of four rooms: the **'Guardaro-** **ba'** (Wardrobe), where, in mid 19th century cabinets, are displayed some object of common use in porcelain and glass; the **King's Study**, with a Biedermeier side table and early nineteenth-century *secretaire* in mahogany, the neo-rococo showcase from Piacenza and the bookcase from the Royal Palace in Turin; the **Reception Room**, where the portraits of Ferdinando II, of his wife Vittoria della Rovere, of Maria Maddalena of Austria and of Cosimo III are noteworthy, as is the furniture from the Royal Palace in Turin, specially made for the royals in the neo-rococo style they were particularly fond of; the **King's Bedroom**, furnished in simple and functional fashion, with iron bed, two chests of Emilian manufacture, *dormeuse*, sofa and armchairs all mid 19th century. The paintings, too, are 19th century, except for the two portraits on the left wall, depicting the Medici popes Leo X and Clement VII, coming from to the Giovian Series in the Uffizi and made by Cristoforo Dell'Altissimo before 1568.

Right,
the Dining Room

Below,
a drawing room

Previous page,
below,
Franciabigio,
*Return of Cicero
from exile,*
in the 'Leo X Room'

**Apartment of the Countess of Mirafiori**. Named after the mistress and then later morganatic wife (from 1869) of Vittorio Emanuele, Rosa Vercellana (the 'Bella Rosina'), ennobled by him with the title of Contessa di Mirafiori, the apartment consists of a **Reception Room**, with neo-classic frescoes on the walls, the work of Luigi Catani, two *consoles* in gilded wood from the early 18th century, sofa of the 'ottoman' type, clock, ground-crystal goblet and porcelain vases, all from the first half of the 19th century. Then comes the **Study**, with bronze and glass chandelier and candlesticks from the mid 19th century, a *dormeuse*, a centre table and *secretaire*, coming respectively from Turin, Modena and Parma, all from the first half of the 19th century. A corridor frescoed in the neo-classic lead to the **Bedroom of the 'Bella Rosina'**, furnished in 1865 to receive the King's partner, with bed with baldachin, furniture and paintings all from the early 19th century. The walls are entirely lined in flow-

er-patterned fabric, draped like radii on the ceiling, so as to allow a glimpse, through a veil of *tulle*, of the pre-existing fresco in the centre. The tour of the first floor ends with the handsome **Bathroom** in Empire style, done for Elisa Baciocchi before 1814, designed by the Court architect Giuseppe Cacialli, who had it dec-

55

tions of still-lifes that once decorated the Villas di Castello, della Topaia and dell'Ambrogiana, today split among the Depositi of Palazzo Pitti and other State Galleries in Florence.

### OUTSIDE GARDEN AND PARK

Coming out of the villa, on the left side looking at the facade, one comes, at a lower ground-level floor, upon the **Large kitchen**. The building, which it is planned to open to the public, was built to the design of Gherardo Mechini at the beginning of the 17th century. Linked to the underground of the villa (the so-called 'cryptoporticus') by a corridor, through which passed the various services provided by the huge and unique kitchen, it is an exceptionally well preserved example – despite its present state of neglect – of architecture built to serve the manifold needs of the Court. The kitchen is flanked, in fact, by various laundry rooms, while through the back courtyard it was originally connected to the stables and coachhouses (now dwellings). A garden of aromatic and medicinal herbs, in part replanted on the northeast side, it was in the area enclosed by the boundary wall to allow easy access to the pot-herbs necessary for cooking.

orated with the mythological scene of *Achilles immersed in the river Lethe* and *Tethys attending the departure of Achilles*.

### SECOND FLOOR

Above,
the Room
of the *papiers peints*

Below,
Bartolomeo Bimbi,
*Cherries,*
in the Still-life Rooms

**Still-life Rooms**. Recently arranged to hold the large paintings by Bartolomeo Bimbi of various species of fruit, the rooms forms the initial core of the Still-life Museum being created. Other rooms on this floor will be given over to it. The museum project plans to bring together at Poggio a Caiano the nuclei of the collec-

Proceeding on the same side one comes on the **Tennis Room**. So called from its being used for the game, it was built at the end of the 18th century as an addition to the other three bulwarks put up in the mid 16th century at the corners of the vast walled area surrounding the villa. It is used as a storehouse.

One continues on the side of the garden looking downhill, from

where there is a fine view on Cascine di Tavola below and Prato plain as far as the Calvana hills and to the more distant Apennines. One goes down to the **English Park**. Created during the second Lorraine period and laid out again after the Unification of Italy by the Amministrazione di Casa Reale. It is decorated with a neoclassic tempietto, by a tableau in brick and stucco and a sculptural group in terracotta depicting the myth of *Ambra and Ombrone*. The visit ends in the **Italian Garden**. Corresponding to the six-teenth-century garden designed by Niccolò Tribolo along with the grandioso building of the Stables below (now municipal property and visitable separately from the villa), it is flanked by the neo-classic 'Stanzone', the large houses for citrus fruit, built by Pasquale Poccianti around 1825.

On the opposite side is the ruin that once held the Roundabout belonging to the Amusement Park conceived by Giovan Battista Ruggeri at the end of the 18th century, still in existence, the reconstruction of which is planned.

An air view of the villa

# Villa di Cerreto Guidi

*Mario Scalini*

Situated on of a hill not far from the Fucecchio marsh in the direction of Florence, the complex of buildings that characterises the fort of Cerreto Guidi stands on the site of an ancient castle once the property of the counts Guidi, an illustrious Tuscan family from which the composite place-name that includes Cerreto, which itself recurs in a document of 780 A. D. dealing with the donation by three noble brothers from Pisa of a small church, in Greti, to the Benedictines of San Savino near Calci. Within original defensive wall, the outlines of which can still be traced in the plan of the whole and is easily made out from above, stands the Romanesque chapel of San Leonardo, close to which Cosimo de' Medici, duke of Florence and Siena at the time, built a hunting lodge of a quite functional kind but freighted with symbolic meaning as outpost of the new centralised power. It is

### HOW TO GET THERE

From Florence take the dual carriageway in the direction of Pisa-Livorno and turn-off at Empoli. Go on towards Vinci and then Cerreto. The villa is in the centre of this town.
*Address* Piaza Umberto I, Cerreto Guidi, (Florence).
*Tel* +39 0571 55707
*Opening time* 8:15-18:30.
Closed the second and third Monday of the month.
*Entry* € 2.00 (full); € 1.00 (reduced).

perhaps no accident that in the simplicity of the ground-plan one finds features spoken of by the Sienese architect Pietro G. Cataneo in his treatise of 1554 (*I quattro primi libri di architettura [...]*), printed in Venice and very up-to-date at the time when the city of Cerreto was conquered (1555) and building began on the 'palazzo' that the documents tell us was "given walls again" in 1566. At that time Bernardo Buontalenti (born in 1523) was little more than forty and is quite probable that the design was his, given that the particular character of the front entry ramp *'a scalera'* (with steps) to be found in other civilian and military buildings conceived by him. The building, supervised by a certain David Fortuni,

Giuseppe Zocchi,
*The Royal Villa
di Cerreto*

a former collaborator of Tribolo, was to take a long time, given that in 1575 Bernardo handed 'the work' on to Alfonso Parigi the Elder, likely responsible for the completion of the complex.

The distribution of the rooms, four together along each side of the ground-floor and upper hall, traversable in sequence and all 'of passage' according to the custom of the time, reveal how the spaces

were meant to lodge several gentlemen with their retinues, and perhaps, if required also animals and families in the ground-floor hall. It is for that reason lower than the other rooms, so that it could be layered with straw, good for lying on and useful to stop mud and dust getting into the adjacent rooms.

On the upper floor, reached by two flights of stairs, the first of which shorter than the second, there is a similar arrangement of rooms but all on the same level, as well a number of passages giving access to two symmetrical loggias corresponding to those on the ground floor, also with triple archways, that give movement to the rear facade, opening onto a square courtyard now in part transformed into a raised garden, but which was once meant to receive riders, packs of hounds and the carriages of the retinue. It is not difficult to imagine the arrival of the hunters nor the piles of game under the porticos with the work they required and the following banquets, prepared in the open air, given the absence of large kitchens.

There will have been a more residential arrangement at the time the villa came down to cardinal Leopoldo de' Medici, as we are told by a document from the State Archive (1671) relating to the passage of the property, which had already belonged to Don Giovanni de' Medici, to Don Pietro and to Don Lorenzo (†1644). When the administration of the Hapsburg Lorraine settled the transfer of the villa, on 29 May 1780, its value was established at 4,740 scudi and the sale to the Tonini family of Pistoia went through. From 1821 it belonged to the Maggi family of Leghorn, who

The stairways
by Buontalenti

built the carriageway that leads to the space in front of the Chapel of San Leonardo, endowed at that time with the massive portico that links the body of the villa to the so-called 'farm'.

Having passed to the marquis Geddes da Filicaja of Florence in 1885, the villa was refurbished and the painter Ruggero Focardi was commissioned to decorate the first room one comes to on

the visit (going immediately left in clockwise direction) where the other country dwellings of the family are reproduced. Bought in 1966 by Galliano Boldrini, it was donated to the state three years later on condition that it become a National Museum.

One can get an idea of the present plan thanks to a three-dimensional model set out in the next room along with plans and eighteenth-century architectural drawings (one of which gives the plan of the villa) donated by the antiquary Alberto Bruschi. Thanks to the overall view one gets a better idea of the natural vocation of the site, inseparably linked

surrounding environment has changed between the 16th century and today as a result of the reclamation that has progressively reduced the natural habitat of the bird species usually present in the marsh. Today the

A perspective view of the stairways by Buontalenti

to fact of the marsh and of hunting. There is a scale-model of the countryside, offering a slice of the area in the direction of the wetlands, seen from the viewer's standpoint, that makes more comprehensible the maps on the walls giving an idea of how the

marsh is under the watchful eye of the Research, Documentation and Promotion of the Marsh of Fucecchio Centre, with headquarters in Larciano (Pistoia). Our knowledge of what it was like to live in the spaces now turned into museum is based on few emains of the Geddes (two round ofas arranged on the ground and first floors) and on the documentary evidence offered by he archives. The oldest inventory relating to the furnishings of the villa (1667) (Archivio di Stato of Florence, Guardaroba Medici, n. 779), lists a fair quanity of paintings: landscapes, ousts, some Medici portraits of he sons of Cosimo II, among hem one by Valore Casini, a *Saint Catherine 'of the wheel'* by Alessandro Allori, a *Saint Barbara* by Matteo Rosselli and even ome nude paintings such as "A mall oil on canvas in chiaroscuro 2/3 cubits high 1 3/4 cubits wide with a nude woman with harp aid to be by Andrea del Sarto...". The furniture is simple, and of ignificance, apart from a 'trucco', the forerunner of the billiard able, is a 'Studiolo', or cabinet of ebony and granatiglio with orass finishings and, going by the transcription provided by Daniela Mignani, "Eight small walnut tools with seats and backs of red cowhide made in Genoa with the H. M. coat of arms on the back" with "Twelve walnut chairs with eats and back of cowhide made n Genoa with backs gilded with he H. M. coat of arms". Few weapons: "Four walnut weapon acks 5 cubit's high"; "Eighteen big-stickers [wild boar] with staff and fringes..."; "Three munitions muskets"; "A musket stock without barrel"; "Four powder flasks and four large flasks for musket", out also "Two carbines or wheel harquebuses" and "A... wheel [pistol] with its stock", all meant for hunting.

The most representative ornament was undoubtedly tapestries, ome portieres with the Medici amily coat of arms, like many still surviving in Florentine collections, and, scattered over the villa's fourteen bedrooms: "Fortyeight pieces of tapestry cloth with hunts and undergrowth... six cubits" tall [about four metres twenty] and another four with

undergrowth and animals that "turn cubits 30" (about 21 metres, lining a whole room therefore). Two bore complex scenes with monarchs, while for the great hall on the first floor two figured tapestries with the Medici coat of arms are mentioned, but not better

Above, the façade of the villa

Below, the front facing the garden

Above,
the ground floor
room

Below,
a fresco depicting
*The villas
of the Geddes
da Filicaja family*,
a work by Ruggero
Focardi (detail)

brought from the 'Guardaroba' of the Florentine Superintendence: four tapestries with the seasons, woven with silver, by the grand-ducal tapestry factory headed at the time by Jacob Eber van Asselt, and then by Pietro Fevére, as well as some seventeenth-century furniture, including the 'lyre' table in the same room and which well represents the typology of those in use in the Medici administrative offices and can still be matched today in the Florentine Superintendences. Set out in various rooms and chosen by analogy with those mentioned in the *Inventory* there are the furniture coming from the bequest – in 1884 – by the antiquary Antonio Conti. Among them is a cabinet in ebonised pear wood and another with polychrome glass inlays and two clocks, one of which a wood 'nocturne' splendidly decorated with the myth of *Pan and Syrinx*, these, too, on the upper floor.

Other pieces of furniture, in the room next to the one with the tapestries, come from the collection of the antiquary Stefano Bardini and his son Ugo, bought by the state in 1996. They include the large finely inlaid *credenza* sixteenth-century in style, next to a cabinet, quite austere, but all gilded, that constitutes a fine *trait-d'union* between the original furniture and that reinvented in late Romanticism.

In the mid 19th century, in fact, there was a vogue for tales like that of the unfortunate Isabella de' Medici, who is alleged to have been strangled (1576) by her husband, Paolo Giordano Orsini (of whom there is a full-length portrait with plumed hat to the side) in a ground-floor room nearby where a bed with baldachin that

described (perhaps the *Stories of Latona*, mother of Apollo and Diana, a deity appropriate to hunting lodge), one of 7 1/2 cubits by five wide and one of 9 1/2 by 6, in which one might otherwise recognise two of the arrases on Stradano cartoons with the famous *Hunts*. Hence the presence in the museum of some similar tapestries, testifies to that taste has found fitting place. It is accompanied by the upper part of a cabinet 'a bambocci' with supporting herms, in the French manner, that is unrestrained in its reconstructive invention.

The wall decoration in the last ground-floor room imitates neoclassic feeling and might date, despite some clumsy changes, to a commission from the Maggi, while the furniture there comes from the Pitti Grand-ducal Guardaroba, since it is still not possible to trace its original presence in the Medici palace or other villas.

In the middle of the main room on the upper floor, corresponding to the ground-floor hall, stand some showcases, again coming from the Royal palace of Pitti, and two large sofas from the Restoration period. All the rooms are divided with mirrored ornaments made in the mid 19th century but done late neo-classic taste, like the *trompe-l'œuil* scene of ruins in the north loggia. There is a considerable and significant number of Medici portraits, among which stands, in the stairwell, the full-length figure of Cosimo I wearing the robes for his coronation as Grand-duke (5 March 1570), perhaps by the Casinis, and another, again full-length, of Don Francesco de' Medici in tournament corselet (c. 1615).

From 28 September 2002, the Villa will house the **Museo storico della caccia e del territorio** (Historical Museum of Hunting and Territory) a monothematic collection of weapons, mainly from hunting and shooting, chosen over almost three decades out of those handed into the police and otherwise destined to destruction, to which have

been added some donations, and temporary loans, some from private individuals, and some noteworthy pieces from the 'Bardini Inheritance' bought by the state in 1996, including the grand-ducal hunting lodge of Pietro Leopoldo or of Ferdinando III of Hapsburg Lorraine.

The arms, displayed in showcases designed at the beginning of the 19th century by the Rangoni company (still in business and now entrusted with their restora-

tion) to safeguard the precious objects and porcelains of the Museo degli Argenti of Palazzo Pitti, are concentrated on the first floor, except for a small nucleus, arranged in the ground-floor 'Room of tapestries'. It consists of knives, hunting-knives, civilian and military knives, mostly from before the 19th century.

A room of Museo storico della caccia e del territorio

# Other Medici Villas
# in Tuscany

# Villa del Trebbio

**HOW TO GET THERE**

North of Florence, close to San Piero a Sieve. From Florence take the via Bolognese for Borgo San Lorenzo; before getting to San Piero a Sieve take the road in the direction of Barberino di Mugello and follow the signs.
*Address* via del Trebbio 1, San Piero a Sieve, Florence.
*Tel* +39 055 8458793 / 8456230
*Opening times* only by appointment for groups up to a maximum of 30 people.
*Entry* € 12.00.

Set on a hilltop in the Apennines north of Florence, a few miles west of San Piero a Sieve, Villa del Trebbio is one of the oldest villas built by the Medici, who came from the Mugello and chose their native region for their first villas. The head of the Medici clan, Giovanni di Bicci, owned the property from the late 14th century, and upon his death in 1428, the villa was inherited by Cosimo the Elder, who commissioned Michelozzo di Bartolomeo to rebuild the original castle.

Set in an excellent strategic position, dominating the Sieve Valley below and near a cross roads (Trebbio derives from the Latin *trivium*), the castle was surrounded by woods and a huge estate which bordered on the Cafaggiolo property.

Although Vasari suggests otherwise, Trebbio was the first of the Mugello castles to be rebuilt by Michelozzo. Immediately after 1428, the building work began, incorporating the existing watchtower into a solid, compact defensive construction surrounded by a moat and drawbridge. The defensive role was necessary on account of the castle's position, however novel features were also introduced to satisfy the requirements of the patron. The walled garden set on two terraces to the right is noteworthy as it was among the first of its kind to be designed for a villa. The upper terrace of the well-preserved garden, a veritable *hortus conclusus*, is decorated with a long pergola made up of a double row of columns with sandstone capitals in various styles (ionic and decorated with foliage motifs), which support a thick covering of vines. As can be seen in the lunette paint-

Justus Utens,
*Il Trebbio,*
1599-1602;
Florence, Museo storico topografico 'Firenze com'era'

Previous pages, the façade of Villa di Cafaggiolo

ed by Justus Utens between 1599 and 1602, there was a second pergola (now lost) on the lower terrace, which retains the original layout of a vegetable garden with a pond, as well as planting de-signed by Michelozzo to satisfy not only defensive requirements, but also Cosimo's spiritual desire for a contemplative life.

Although Cosimo always kept abreast of the political develop-

The right side of Villa del Trebbio, with the pergola

A detail
of the pergola

The villa, later inherited by Cosimo I's descendants, was enlarged when Ferdinando I purchased other farms, and was sold in 1644 by Ferdinando II to the Florentine Giuliano Serragli. The latter bequeathed it to the Fathers of the Oratory and following subsequent changes of hands it was sold to the Scaretti family, the present owners.

Since the time Utens executed his lunette, various changes have been made to the villa: the farmhouses adjoining the villa and in a line along the large central space (transformed into a cypress grove in the 19th century), have been pulled down.

In place of the vegetable plots on the lawn in front of the villa, there is now a twentieth-century box hedge and rose garden. Michelozzo's original design remains largely unchanged, retaining the imposing square plan crowned by corbels, inner courtyard with a well, the walled garden and the chapel.

ments in Florence, he retreated to Mugello to enjoy the intellectual company of his circle of humanists and to pursue his interest in agriculture: grafting and pruning fruit trees, a technique at which he excelled.

## Cosimo I from Mugello to Firenze

Following the meteoric rise of the Medici family, Giovanni di Bicci, left his inheritance to his eldest son, Cosimo I, the *pater patriae*. Upon the death of his brother Lorenzo (1440), his nephew Pierfrancesco was orphaned at only ten years old and Cosimo took over the administration Pierfrancesco's inheritance. In 1451, when he reached maturity, Villa del Trebbio and its estate, passed to the cadet branch of the family.

Legend has it that the seventeen year-old Cosimo de' Medici was at Trebbio with his mother, Maria Salviati, Giovanni dalle Bande Nere's widow, when he received the news of the assassination of duke Alessandro de' Medici in January 1537. With the extinction of the main Medici line, the 'glories' of the family were rekindled from Trebbio when Cosimo de' Medici, an ambitious young man made a hasty return to Florence; the glories of the dynasty continued for two centuries, until the extinction of the Medici family upon the death of Giangastone in 1737.

# Villa di Cafaggiolo

The most illustrious Medici residence in Mugello is situated on the old road from Florence to Bologna, a short distance from the turning to Trebbio.

In the family since the mid fourteenth century, Vasari records that Cosimo commissioned Michelozzo to rebuild the villa in the 1430's: "On the advice and to the designs of Michelozzo, Cosimo de' Medici carried out building work on the Cafaggiuolo palazzo in Mugello, turning it into a fortress surrounded by a moat; he built the farms, roads, gardens, fountains and woods around the villa as well as other features of a stately home". Vasari's description clearly shows

**HOW TO GET THERE**

From Florence take the via Bolognese for Borgo San Lorenzo and then for Barberino di Mugello, the castle stands 2 km along the main road.
*Address* via Nazionale 16, Barberino di Mugello, Florence. *Tel* +39 055 8479293 / 8456230 or 8479293
Opening times subject to seasonal variation: Sat and Sun 10-12.30 / 14:30-18:30; only in the summer period (from 15 April to 15 October) open also Wed and-Fri 14.30-18.30 (only the ground-floor of the villa).
*Entry* € 12,00.
Only by booking groups can visit all the villa and the park (tel 055 8479293 / 8456230).

The façade
of the villa

Justus Utens, *Villa di Cafaggiolo*, 1599-1602;
Florence, Museo storico topografico 'Firenze com'era'

the renaissance evolution of the original castle and the two-fold role of fortress and villa desired by Cosimo: a defensive castle in the wild lands to the North of Florence, but also a country house, ideally situated for hunting and surrounded by vegetable gardens and ornamental gardens decorated with fountains, as can be seen in the lunette painted by Justus Utens.

From the start, the Medici used Cafaggiolo principally as a summer residence and the villa was particularly dear to Lorenzo de' Medici. Lorenzo's guests included Pico della Mirandola, Marsilio Ficino and Agnolo Poliziano, who, as tutor to Lorenzo the Magnificent's children, taught the humanities to the future pope Leo X. Cosimo I, who inherited Cafaggiolo in 1537, enlarged the

Here and at the previous page above, the villa and the stable building

### 'La Nencia da Barberino'

Tradition has it that Lorenzo the Magnificent, a poet and man of letters, as well as a master politician, wrote his famous pastoral poem *La Nencia da Barberino*, in praise of the area's beauty, while at Cafaggiolo. The realistic and touching praise bestowed by the farmer Vallera on his Nencia, "white and red and shapely", "so light yet so striking, that she opens up the hearts of many", reflect, albeit ironically, the aspirations to simplicity and the country life, which Leon Battista Alberti described in his treatise the *Family*, and which were a characteristic of the Medici throughout the 15th century.

Two interiors
of the villa

time of the Lorraine dynasty. During this period, it also played a strategic role as a staging post on the new postal road opened under the 'illuminated' policy of the Grand-dukes, who improved the road network in the area. In 1864 it was sold by the Italian State to the Borghese princes, who carried out radical changes, demolishing one of the towers, filling in the moat around the villa and opening a large entrance arch in the surrounding walls.

Numerous features of Michelozzo's architectural design survive in the interior, such as the ornamental motifs on the entrance door on the ground floor and the various types of sandstone pedestals and capitals. The long, sixteenth-century stables on the left survive, whereas the formal garden decorated with fountains, seen in Utens' lunette behind the villa, is now a park containing mature trees.

villa and built a large, walled hunting reserve which he filled with a variety of rare animals. Used as a hunting lodge by both Francesco I and Ferdinando I, who stayed for long periods in the autumn, the villa was mainly a holiday residence until the

# Villa di Careggi

Bought by Giovanni di Bicci de' Medici in 1417 for 800 gold florins, this old nobleman's palace, which had belonged to Tommaso Lippi, was redesigned for Cosimo the Elder by his favourite architect, Michelozzo di Bartolomeo, in the first half of the 15th century. The severe appearance of the building, with the open battlemented gallery reminiscent of military architecture, contrasted with the natural landscape, described by Giovanni Villani as among the most 'delightful' near Florence. The reached, lying just outside the city walls. The position of the villa meant that Cosimo often took refuge at Careggi, surrounding himself with artists, philosophers and men of letters, such as, Donatello, Brunelleschi and Poliziano, and turning the villa into the headquarters of the Platonic Academy founded by Marsilio Ficino. The cultivated circle of erudite scholars continued to meet at the villa under Piero the Gouty and Lorenzo the Magnificent, who both, like Cosimo the Elder, died at Careggi. After their

**HOW TO GET THERE**

Within the area occupied by the hospital of the same name. Follow the signs for Ospedale di Careggi.
*Owners* Azienda Ospedaliera di Careggi.
*Address* Viale Pieraccini 17, Florence.
*Bus* 14 C
*Tel* +39 055 4279497
*Opening times* 9-17; Sat 9-13; closed Sun.
*Entry* free.
To visit the villa permission is required from the direction of the Azienda Ospedaliera di Careggi.

Medici bought up surrounding farms to make the villa the centre of an agricultural estate, similar in many aspects to the two Mugello villas, but differing from these in that Careggi was easily deaths, the villa fell into decline and was set on fire in 1529 by republican enemies of the Medici. After the Medici returned to power the duke Alessandro undertook large-scale restoration and redec-

Villa di Careggi, the front

Right,
the small
Ionic loggia

Below,
the South front
of the villa

Next page, above,
a general view
of the front
with the small Ionic
loggia

## Anti-Medici fires

After the deposition of the Medici by the populace in April 1527 and the restoration of the Republic, there was a strong reaction against Medici power, which was represented by Giuliano's, duke of Nemours, and Lorenzo's, duke of Urbino, natural sons, Ippolito and Alessandro, and by their tutor, cardinal Giulio de' Medici. After Palazzo Medici in Florence was saved from destruction in 1529, it was impossible to stop the *Arrabbiati* (a 'young brigade', led by Dante and Lorenzo da Castiglione, intent on "burning and destroying their enemies" houses and villas) from setting fire to Villa di Careggi. Medici revenge didn't take long: thanks to the alliance of Giulio, who became pope Clement VII, with Charles V, emperor of the Sacred Roman Empire, the democratic Republic of Florence fell definitively in the summer of 1530, and the Medici dynasty was restored under Alessandro.

oration work, commissioning Pontormo in 1535 to decorate a loggia with allegorical scenes (now lost). Helped by Bronzino, Pontormo completed the work in 1536,

a few days before the Duke was assassinated, which put an end to further work to the villa. In 1609, Giovan Carlo inherited the villa from his father Ferdinando I. The fascinating underground grotto, decorated with calcareous sponges and wall paintings, as well as the frescoes in the ground floor 'Reception Room' and in the 'stanzone', where citron plants were stored, date to this period.

The villa, which had become too expensive to maintain, was sold by the Lorraine family in 1779, at the same time as many other properties, such as Cerreto Guidi, Artimino and Castelmartini. Bought by Vincenzo Orsi, in 1848 it passed into the hands of Francis Joseph Sloane, a scholar and collector, who transformed the garden and commissioned the

neo-Medieval decorations in the interior. The villa had many other proprietors before it was bought by Florence hospital, the present owners.

The 'stanzone', where citrus plants were stored

# Villa Medici in Fiesole

**HOW TO GET THERE**

In the immediate neighbourhood of Fiesole.
*Address* via Beato Angelico 2, Fiesole (Florence). *Bus 7*
*Fax* +39 055 2398994
*Opening time* 9-13; closed Sat and Sun (by appointment)
*Entry*: € 6,00

In the mid 15th century, Cosimo de' Medici and his second son Giovanni bought a 'gentleman's residence', known as 'Belcanto', from Niccolò Baldi, and commissioned the family architect, Michelozzo di Bartolomeo, to transform it into a Renaissance house.

According to Vasari, Michelozzo showed his brilliance in successfully solving the problem posed by the steep hill on which he was to build the extension to the villa, by arranging the design over more than one level. The lower vaulted level was set aside for "cellars, stables, storerooms and other handsome and useful accessories", whereas the upper level was devoted to bedrooms, drawing rooms and rooms for "books and others for music". The result was such that this 'magnificent and grand palace', in which the Medici had invested heavily, was in such perfect condition in the mid sixteenth century when Vasari was writing that it had not "ever lost a single hair".

The novelty of Michelozzo's design, in term of the previous residences of Trebbio, Cafaggiolo and Careggi, still medieval in style, lies in the perfectly orthogonal ground-plan and in cubic volume of the structure, within which the two loggias are inserted.

The unique position of the villa, with its open loggias stretching out to the countryside below and overlooking the various levels of

Beside,
a view of the villa from the upper garden

Next page,
the buttress of the upper garden

the hanging garden, together with its library and art collections, bear witness to the idea of the villa as a place for contemplative rest and intellectual pleasure, rather than as the centre of an agricultural estate, which was a frequent characteristic of other Medici villas. Giovanni de' Medici, a singlar character devoted to pleasure but also a patron of artists such as Donatello and Filippo Lippi and a learned bibliophile, who commissioned it, certainly had a hand in this.
The villa, which outstripped Careggi to become a focal point for a large group of humanists gravitating around the Medici Court, was much loved by Lorenzo the Magnificent, who invited Poliziano, Pico della Miran-

## The 'Pazzi Conspiracy'

In 1478 the anti-Medici plot, which became famous as the 'Pazzi Conspiracy' was hatched. The main conspirators were Jacopo and Francesco de' Pazzi, Francesco Salviati and the young cardinal Raffaello Riario, a descendant of pope Sixtus IV. Riario and Jacopo de' Pazzi had been invited to a sumptuous banquet by Lorenzo and Giuliano de' Medici, which should have been held on 25 April at Villa Medici in Fiesole, and the occasion was to have been used to poison the two brothers.
However Giuliano was indisposed and the plot was postponed. The 'conspiracy' was put into action the next day, 26 April 1478, during Mass in the Florentine cathedral of Santa Maria del Fiore: Giuliano de' Medici was killed but the conspirators failed: they were all captured and put to death on the insistence of the populace.

Above,
the entrance
to the lower garden

Beside,
the villa overlooking
the garden

dola, Cristoforo Landino to congregate here.

This group of thinkers and men of letters held readings, recitals and erudite discussions here, thus increasing knowledge of classical culture, which was the hinge for the artistic and literary renewal of the Renaissance. Although the villa was much-loved by the Medici between the 15th and 16th centuries, later generations did not lavish the same attention upon it.

Soon after acceding to the throne, Cosimo III de' Medici sold it in 1671 to Cosimo del Sera for 4,000 florins. Bought in 1722 by Lady Orford, who commissioned the architect Gaspero Paoli to carry out radical changes to the original building, it was sold in the 19th century to William Spence, and later to Lady Sybil Cutting in 1909, and in 1959 to its current owners, the Mazzini Marchi family.

The garden was redesigned by the landscape gardener Cecil Pinsent, who worked for Lady Cutting between 1911 and 1923, restructuring the villa and creating a neo-fifteenth-century garden on the lower terrace.

A view of the lower garden

# Villa di Collesalvetti

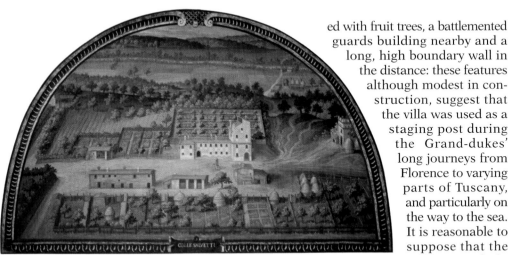

ed with fruit trees, a battlemented guards building nearby and a long, high boundary wall in the distance: these features although modest in construction, suggest that the villa was used as a staging post during the Grand-dukes' long journeys from Florence to varying parts of Tuscany, and particularly on the way to the sea. It is reasonable to suppose that the painting was faithful to its subject, since Justus Utens travelled to all of the villas he painted, taking measurements and notes on the buildings he was to represent. The 14 lunettes, the only iconographic collection of Medici property, therefore have great documentary importance, particularly in cases such as Collesalvetti, where radical transformations have left little of the original structure.

The property was enlarged in 1571, when the commendatory abbot of the Collesalvetti community gave the neighbouring estate belonging to the Badia to Eleonora of Toledo, wife of Cosimo I, in perpetual emphyteusis. Collesalvetti villa-farmhouse is unrecognisable today as it is incorporated into the town of Collesalvetti; the villa passed into private hands in the past and is still privately owned.

**HOW TO GET THERE**

In the centre town of Collesalvetti (Leghorn).

Included by Utens among the most important Medici properties in his series of lunettes painted for Ferdinando I, Villa di Collesalvetti, set on Monte Pisano, which once belonged to the Salvetti family, was owned by the Medici from the time of Cosimo the Elder.

In his lunette formerly at Artimino and now in the 'Firenze com'era' Museum, the Flemish painter represented the villa at the centre of a vast agricultural estate. The villa, with an older towered section, is shown set in countryside which spreads out in fields and woods and is surrounded by rigorously defined farms, farm buildings, barns, stables and store rooms for carts and farm equipment. Other features represented by Utens include a large fenced garden beside the villa, which is divided into flowerbeds and plant-

Justus Utens,
*Villa di Colle Salvetti,*
1599-1602;
Florence, Museo storico topografico 'Firenze com'era'

# Villa di Agnano

Set in the Pisan Valdarno (Arno valley), near San Giuliano Terme, Villa di Agnano was built by Lorenzo the Magnificent after 1486. The position on the slopes of Monte Pisano, in an area fed by water from springs in Asciano and facing a rich, partly marshy plain irrigated by the Vicinaia, made the villa and surrounding estate ideal for holidays and particularly for hunting expeditions. The land was bought from the Agnano Olivetan monks and reclaimed by Lorenzo, who in this way, "made a useful possession by drying marshes and watery places to the great benefit of those around". The building work was well-advanced by 1489, when the villa already had a "courtyard with loggias", "vegetable gardens and lawns" and pigeon and chicken houses on the farms, but had not been completed when Lorenzo died in 1492, although it had been inhabitable and Lorenzo stayed here more than once on 1491.

A later drawing by Giovan Battista da Sangallo shows the villa as it must have appeared when it was inherited by Piero de' Medici. Arranged along a symmetrical axis perpendicular to the main façade and connected to the farm buildings behind, the villa had a loggia at the rear giving onto a walled garden divided into four sections, which in turn continued into the large pond-hatchery. After the expulsion of Piero from Florence, it was sold in 1494 with the Volterra estate of Spedaletto, to Francesco Cybo Orsini, who left it to his son cardinal Innocenzo in 1519; it later passed, by Cybo Malaspina, dukes of Massa, to Este of Modena.

At the time of Ferdinando Carlo Hapsburg Lorraine, who inherited it from his mother Maria Beatrice on the extinction of the Este family, the belvedere terrace on the side towards the garden and the romantic park were executed to designs by the gardener Maximilian Hahn, who changed the original Renaissance garden plan. Sold in 1889 by Francesco Ferdinando Hapsburg Lorraine to Oscar Tobler, the villa is still owned by the latter's heirs, the Tadini Buoninsegni Tobler family.

## HOW TO GET THERE

From Florence take the dual carriageway Firenze-Pisa-Livorno and turn-off at Cascina. From there go on in the direction of Caprona and then Calci and on to Agnano. The villa lies north west of Agnano.
*Address* via 25 aprile 34, Agnano (Pisa).
*Tel* +39 050 856353
*Opening times* only by appointment.
*Entry* free.

A general view of Villa di Agnano

# Villa di Spedaletto

**HOW TO GET THERE**

From Pontedera take the state road in the direction of Volterra and follow the signs directing to Lajatico. The villa is not open to the public.

Lorenzo the Magnificent bought the Spedaletto estate in the vicinity of Volterra in 1486, the year the Knights of Altopascio granted him in emphyteusis the Pisan estate of Agnano and an old palace known as the 'Ospedale dei Santi Ippolito e Cassiano', together with its land. After the capture of Volterra in 1472, which was taken mainly in order to control the alum mines, the Medici became interested in the area on account of the healing thermal waters at

Bagno a Morba, which Lorenzo's mother, Lucrezia Tornabuoni, rented from the Knights of Monte from 1478.

The Spedaletto estate, which included approximately twenty plots of land, was reorganised by Lorenzo the Magnificent immediately upon its purchase by planting new crops: vines and pastureland. The old 'Ospedale' was transformed into a 'gentleman's residence' between 1487 and 1491, during which period Lorenzo visited often while taking the waters at Morba to cure his gout and, as he wrote to his daughter Contessina, "becoming as healthy as I ever was, praise God".

The design incorporated pre-existing buildings, including a

solid tower, into the new parts to create a square plan villa with an inner courtyard decorated with a loggia, and an unusual 'Reception Room' on the ground floor giving on to one side of the courtyard. It is thought that Simone del Pollaiolo, known as Il Cronaca, was involved in the project as there is documentary evidence that he was at Spedaletto in 1490. The simple, functional architecture of the country villa were offset by the magnificence of the pictorial decoration commissioned between 1490 and 1491 by Lorenzo who wanted to create villa of delights. The involvement of great artists, such as Domenico Ghirlandaio, Filippino Lippi, Pietro Perugi-

no, and above all, Sandro Botticelli, who "worked much at Spedaletto in Volterra" (Vasari), gives an idea of the importance of the lost fresco cycle representing mythological scenes in the loggia and the large reception room on the ground floor. Ghirlandaio executed the *Story of Vulcan* with "many nude figures making arrows for Jove with hammers".

After Lorenzo's death in 1492, the villa-farm of Spedaletto was sold by his son Piero to Francesco Cybo in 1494, together with the Agnano estate. In 1606 Alberigo Cybo Malaspina sold the villa to senator Bartolomeo Corsini and it has remained in the Corsini family ever since.

Above and at the previous page, the main façade of the villa

# Villa di Camugliano

**HOW TO GET THERE**

From Florence take the dual carriageway Firenze-Pisa-Livorno to Pontedera est turn-off and from there go on south in the direction of Capannori. The villa is not open to the public.

Villa di Camugliano lies east of Ponsacco (Pisa), near a small rural, originally feudal, hamlet. This area, at the foot of the hills spanning the Era and Cascina valleys, has been inhabited since the 9th century.

The construction of this grand house at the centre of a vast estate, was begun by duke Alessandro de' Medici as part of his policy of territorial expansion towards the Pisa plain, and was completed by Cosimo I.

The villa, reached a spectacular avenue of cypress trees, dominates the surrounding area. At the centre of the lawn in front of the compact square villa, with four corner towers, is Giovanni Bandini's sixteenth-century statue of *Hercules killing the Hydra*, as solitary and impressive as a tutelary deity.

The need to combine defensive with residential requirements is obvious in the numerous features of fortified architecture: the solid scarp wall, the corner reinforcements at the base of the towers, and the huge area in front of the villa, delimited by two symmetrical buildings used either as stables or barracks, which

could be used as a parade ground. The anti-Medici insurrections in Pisa and the Valdarno (Arno valley) communes in 1494 and 1539 made it of utmost importance to create a network of residences with dual military purposes in which to take refuge and defend in times of need; another example is the later Villa dell'Ambrogiana, built in a style reminiscent of Villa di Camugliano.

In the second half of the 16th century, Cosimo I donated the villa to Giuliano Gondi in exchange for services rendered to the Medici family.

Matteo Botti bought the villa from Giuliano Gondi, but when he was created marquis of Campiglia d'Orcia by Cosimo II, he gave the villa back to the Grandduke with an act dated December 25 1615.

On September 23 1637 a concession issued by Ferdinando II definitively renounced the family's claim on the villa and Pisan estate, transferring them to senator Filippo Niccolini, together with the conferral of the title of marquis of Camugliano and Ponsacco. This act was reconfirmed in 1738 by Francesco II of Lor-

The façade overlooking the lawn with the statue of *Hercules killing the Hydra* by Giovanni Bandini

Previous page, the large lawn facing the villa

Right,
a small tower
with a building
in the background
adjoining the villa

Below,
a perspective
of the façade
with one of
the towers
and the central
stairways

raine in respect of Giovan Luca Niccolini. The Niccolini undertook the transformations carried out between the 18th and 19th centuries, such as the double staircase, built to connect the fore- court with a three arch loggia on the first floor (now closed), the English park and the low exedra of greenery which, decorated with marble busts, delimits the grand central forecourt.

The entire building from the outside

# Villa La Topaia

**HOW TO GET THERE**

Near Castello between Sesto Fiorentino and Careggi. It is not open to the public.

A view of the villa from the garden

Set half way up the hill above Villa di Castello and Villa della Petraia, at the foot of Monte Morello, Villa La Topaia was built on the site of a pre-existing farm in the mid 16th century.

Cosimo granted the use of this villa, almost a farm annexe of the two principal villas, to the writers Scipione Ammirato and Benedetto Varchi, who wrote *Storie fiorentine* here. Varchi's description of the place shows that the villa, although small, wanted for nothing: as a 'gentleman's residence', it boasted a large central hall, a chapel, a small loggia, a mezzanine for 'wardrobes', linen rooms and servants, a vegetable garden and a garden with a 'pratello' (lawn). Villa La Topaia, which Varchi referred to as 'Cosmiano' in honour of his patron, was principally used for holidays until the time of Cosimo III, who carried out general renovation, transforming it into a lodge for rest and delight, where he could stay during his frequent visits to the vineyards of Castello and of La Petraia. The Grand-duke, who was a keen natural scientist, increased production in the garden and orchard in order to collect "all the varieties of fruit, citrus, grapes and flowers that have been found to date in the wild, as well as the extraordinary and

bizarre freaks of nature". The Grand-duke was not merely content with his botanical collection in the garden, but also commissioned Bartolomeo Bimbi to execute an important series of botanical paintings to scale and from life, which were kept at the villa. Cosimo III's work on the villa includes the central loggia with decorative motifs leading to the drawing room and the small grotto which leads to the upper level of the garden.

In the first half of the 19th century, the Lorraine family, to whom it passed upon the extinction of the Medici dynasty, divided the villa into two separate parts: one part for the Grand-ducal Court, the other for a family of farmers who worked the land. Vittorio Emanuele III donated the villa to the State, which in turn gave it to the 'Opera Nazionale Combattenti'; the villa was later sold and has been in private hands ever since.

A detail of the façade

# Villa di Seravezza

## HOW TO GET THERE

From Florence take the A11 autostrada (Firenze-Mare), leave the autostrada at the Versilia turn-off and go on along the SP 9 into the centre of Seravezza.
*Address* via del Palazzo 358, Seravezza (Lucca).
*Tel* +39 0584 756100 / 756135
The villa houses the "Museo del lavoro e delle tradizioni popolari della Versilia storica" and puts on exhibitions of modern and contemporary art.
*Opening times* subject to seasonal variation: 15-19:30 (winter opening times); 16-23 (summer opening times); closed Mon.
*Entry* € 3.00 (full); € 2.00 (reduced) – winter tariff; € 5,00 (full); € 3,00 (reduced) – summer tariff.

The Villa di Seravezza is situated between Massa and Pietrasanta (Lucca), at the foot of the Apuan Alps, near the confluence of the Serra and Vezza rivers, which give the place its name. Cosimo I, who was interested in the Captaincy of Seravezza for strategic policy and economic reasons, commissioned an architect in his circle to build the Villa in approximately 1555. There is no documentary evidence pinpointing the architect and the opinion of scholars oscillates between Bartolomeo Ammannati and Bernardo Buontalenti. The Commune of Ser-

Versilia; once under Medici control (1513) it became an important control point for Florentine State territory boundaries. Its economic importance was due to the old marble and silver quarries in the area which had been closed for a time and which Cosimo decided to reopen. The Duke therefore found the silver lead veins in the prized Bottino mine and set it working once again. He also promoted the quarrying of marble, opening the famous quarry of 'mistio' marble, known as 'fior di pesco' (peach blossom) or 'breccia di Seravezza' in 1563. As can

The well

The ashlar worked portal surmounted by the Medici's coat of arms

ravezza was of strategic importance as it had always been at the heart of the conflict between the Republics of Pisa, Genoa, Lucca and Florence for possession of

be seen from Utens' lunette, which represents the villa from the right hand side, Seravezza was in a delightful setting between the woods on Monte Costa and the left bank

of the Vezza, which was crossed by a bridge at that point. The villa was equipped with all elements to make the court's summer visits pleasurable: an enclosed vegetable garden, a "lawn... with a fruit garden", a chapel and a stable block. At the same time, the solid and compact shape of the villa, the acute-angled corners and the slit openings on the ground floor, reveal that the architectural design reflected the need for control and possible defence of the area. Assiduously visited by the Grand-dukes, particularly during the greatest period of mining for Medici breccia, the villa was inhabited by both Francesco I's second wife, Bianca Cappello, and by Cristina Lorraine, the widow of Ferdinando I, who spent several months here each year.

Inherited by the Lorraine family after the end of the Medici dynasty, it was later acquired by the State, which donated it to the Commune of Seravezza in 1861. The Commune initially used the villa as a prison and later as the seat of the Municipality.

Above,
a general view
of the villa

Right above,
Justus Utens,
*Villa di Seravezza,*
1599-1602;
Florence, Museo
storico topografico
'Firenze com'era'

93

# Villa di Stabbia

**HOW TO GET THERE**

From Florence take the carriageway Firenze-Pisa-Livorno and turn off at Empoli. Go on in the direction of Cerreto, and on towards Montecatini.
The villa stands in the centre town of Stabbia (a minor village of Commune of Cerreto). It is not open to the public.

The villa's main front

Villa di Stabbia, set on mount Stabbia near the Cerreto Guidi hills in a panoramic position bordering the vast Fucecchio marsh, is among the large group of villa-farms built up progressively by the Medici in the second half of the 16th century in order to exert both economic and strategic control over the Grand-duchy. The place chosen for this villa had been used by the Republic of Florence since the beginning of the 15th century for hunting abundant and varied wildlife, both birds and fish, in the marsh.
The villa was commissioned by Cosimo I between 1548 and 1568, incorporated a pre-existing fortified building, which had belonged to the Soderini family and was bought by Alessandro de' Medici. It is thought that the transformation of the original "house with a tower, part for the worker, part for the gentleman" into a villa fit to be included among the prestigious Medici properties (with large central hall, ashlar-work doors and mezzanines for the servants), was executed to designs by the versatile Niccolò Tribolo. Helped by Davide Fortini, he was working in the area just before 1550, when he died, on the construction of the banks of Fucecchio Lake.
The new building, described in 1568 among Cosimo I's properties as "a gentleman's palace with a piazza in front of the Lake, and with a small vegetable garden behind and a small stable on the piazza", also had kilns, "workmen's houses" and thirteen farms managed by two stewards. The villa was the administrative centre of Medici property in the marsh area, which included the nearby and grander Villa di Cerreto Guidi.
Cosimo I gave the villa to his sons Don Pietro and cardinal Ferdinando, but it lost importance after the construction of the new Grand-ducal estates in Valdinievole, such as Ponte a Cappiano, Montevettolini, Bellavista and Castelmartini, following the large-scale reclaiming work on the banks of the lake. Following the shrewd management of Don Lorenzo de' Medici, who inherited from his father Ferdinando I in 1606, it was sold by the Lorraine dynasty after 1777, at the same time they sold off the majority of the Grand-ducal land. Since that time it has been radically altered many times and has remained in private hands.

# Villa di Pratolino

One of the grandest Medici villas, Villa di Pratolino was pulled down in the early nineteenth century and its appearance can now only be reconstructed through studying the adjoining buildings that survive, the park, visual and written documents of the past, and, more indirectly, through the works of art and architecture elsewhere that reflects the personality of Francesco I. It was Cosimo I's eldest son who decided to build Pratolino in 1569, while his father was still alive. He chose a plot of land far from Florence in a wild and steep area on the slopes of the Apennines, bought the year before from Benedetto Uguccioni. The 'marvels' of Pratolino were exalted in eulogistic texts and poems before it was even completed, as if to sanction the excessive cost. Bernardo Buontalenti designed the villa, completed in 1575, which cost an exorbitant 782 thousand *scudi*, double the cost of building the Uffizi.

Giambologna, the *Apennines*, c. 1580

Right,
a detail
of the *Apennines*
by Giambologna

Below,
the sculpture-fountain
representing
the *Mugnone river*

Justus Utens' representation of
the villa of 1599 reveals that the
it was the architectonic synthesis of Francesco's character and
interests. It appears as the gen-
erating nucleus of the complex
garden layout, which extends
into the surrounding wild countryside. The longitudinal axis on
which the villa is set begins above
the villa with the *Fountain of
Jove* and the colossal *Apennines*
and ends, via the *'Stradone delle
pile'* (Basin Avenue), at the *Wash-
erwoman Fountain*; the axis opens
out into a network of avenues,
paths and labyrinths, dotted with
grottoes and fountains driven
by sophisticated machines that
created sound and water movement. The lush sublime nature of
the park (*natura naturalis*), transformed by the Prince into a work
of art and architecture (*natura
artificialis*) with the help of artists

## Pratolino at present

Not even the sixteenth-century garden survived changes in taste: in 1818 Ferdinando III created a large English-style park to designs by the Bohemian Joseph Frietsch. In 1872, Pratolino estate was bought by the Russian Demidoff family, who restored the various buildings originally adjoining the villa (the stables, farmhouse and chapel) and added a new wing to transform Buontalenti's 'Paggeria' (servants' quarters) into a house. Since 1981 the estate has been owned by the Province of Florence. Today some exceptional and moving 'marvels' of Pratolino survive, such as the grandiose sculpture-fountain of the *Apennines*, by Giambologna (c. 1580), with the *Dragon* added by Giovan Battista Foggini, with two inner Grottoes and the lake in front; the hexagonal chapel by Buontalenti; the fountain *Mugnone river*; the '*Maschera*' *Fish-pond*; *Cupid's Grotto*. The nineteenth-century landscaped park is the most important in Tuscany.

A view of the park

Above,
Justus Utens,
*Villa di Pratolino*,
1599-1602;
Florence, Museo
storico topografico
'Firenze com'era'

Right,
a general view
of the residence
of the Demidoff
family

such as Giambologna, Bartolomeo Ammannati, Valerio Cioli and Vincenzo Danti, became an expression of his hedonistic and 'bizarre' experimentalism. The unusual combination of nature, art and technology was not confined to the garden: the villa was compact externally and rationally geometric in the symmetry of its internal layout, but adorned with a series of artificial basement grottoes. Of the *Deluge*, *Galathea*, *Stove*, *Sponge* and *Samaritan Grottoes*, it was to the latter that Francesco, quiet and evasive by nature, repaired for secret meetings with his beloved Bianca Cappello.
After the sudden deaths of Francesco and Bianca in 1587, the vil-

la, which was haunted by their troubled and melancholic spirit, was maintained but little visited by their immediate heirs. It was not until a century later that Cosimo III's son, Grand Prince Ferdinando, took this extraordinary place to heart and rekindled the old splendour with new artists (the frescoes and paintings by Pier Dandini, Crescenzio Onofri, Anton Domenico Gabbiani and Sebastiano Ricci), theatrical and musical productions (held in the theatre he built to designs by the architect Antonio Ferri with scenery by Ferdinando Galli from Bibbiena). Progressively abandoned after the death of the Grand Prince (1713), particularly by the new Lorraine dynasty, the villa was damaged by rising damp from the underground grottoes yet no steps were taken to remedy the problem. Arguably the most magnificent, and certainly the most extravagant Medici villa, a "theatre of delights, magnificence and ease", was demolished by Ferdinando III in 1820.

Above,
the chapel built
in 1580
by Bernardo
Buontalenti

Left,
a pond in the park

# Villa di Lappeggi

**HOW TO GET THERE**

Leave the A1
motorway at
Firenze Sud
and follow the signs
for Antella.
From there, going
on in the direction
of Grassina,
after a few kms
one meets
the via di Lappeggi.
The villa is not open
to the public.

Justus Utens,
*Villa La Peggio*,
1599-1602;
Florence, Museo
storico topografico
'Firenze com'era'

An old house which once belonged to the Bardi, set on the top of Lapeggi hill (also known as 'Appeggio' or 'La Peggio') above Antella, passed through the hands of the Gualtierotti, Bartolini Salimbeni and Ricasoli, before it was sold by the latter for thirteen thousand gold florins to prince Francesco de' Medici in 1569.

Redesigned by Bernardo Buontalenti, Villa di Lappeggi appears in Justus Utens' representation dating to the end of the 16th century, as a horseshoe shaped house with a central courtyard closed at the front by a battlemented wall pierced by the entrance gate. The elegant façade is decorated with two orders of loggias. The beauty of its position, close to the town yet in the country, and its use for entertainments and pastimes, such as ball games, or for hunting expeditions, can be seen in the details of Utens' lunette: the villa is surrounded by a walled garden with a lawn and orchard, there are adjoining stables and storerooms, while the typical Florentine hills represented around the villa are dotted with well-cultivated farms.

Ferdinando I, who became Grand-duke after the death of his brother, gave the villa to Francesco's illegitimate son, Don Antonio de' Medici, and it was then owned by Giovanni Antonio Orsini. The villa returned to the Crown in 1640 when Ferdinando II gave it to his brother Don Mattias. Upon the death of Don Mattias, who as governor of Siena only visited infrequently, the villa passed to

Cosimo III's brother, cardinal Francesco Maria, in 1667, which marked the start of a splendid era at Lappeggi.

With the stated intention of emulating the marvels at Pratolino, the court architect, Antonio Ferri was commissioned to restructure the villa. Ferri designed the terraced garden and park, adorn-

tion of the interior, executing one of the most important Florentine rococo pictorial cycles.

The villa was the perfect place for the often excessive receptions, banquets and given by the unorthodox Cardinal. According to descriptions by the poet Giovan Battista Fagiuoli, "outrageous things were said and done" dur-

The monumental stairway of the garden facing the villa

ed with laurel avenues and citrus trees, and decorated with fountains, sculpture and water lilies. The architect also reorganised the various floors of the villa, dividing it into four flats, or 'pavilions', named after the dominant colour of the furnishing fabrics: yellow, turquoise, red and green. In the early 18th century the most famous artists of the time, including Alessandro Gherardini, Pier Dandini and Rinaldo Botti, worked on the decora-

## Carpe diem

Legend has it that Francesco Maria commissioned Antonio Ferri to execute numerous drawings for the restructuring of Lappeggi. Once he had chosen the grandest and asked its price, which amounted to 80.000 *scudi*, he asked the architect, "And if I only wanted to spend 30.000, but keep the same project, how long would the villa last?" Upon Ferri's reply that it would last for 18 years, the Cardinal replied, "Get going then! 18 years is long enough; it will last as long as me".

Above,
a view
of the garden

Above,
Giuseppe Zocchi,
*The Royal Villa
di Lappeggi*

ing the events, which were attended by a diverse crowd of musicians, actors and favourites of the prince. A theatre, 'coffee house' and games room for tennis were also added to the villa. The life of delights and magnificence, at its apex at the time of the visit by Frederick IV, king of Denmark and Norway in 1709, was brought to an abrupt end in 1710 by the death of Francesco Maria, shortly after his unhappy marriage to Eleonora Gonzaga, which had been arranged in the failed hope of ensuring an heir to the dynasty which was threatened by imminent extinction.

Once back in the hands of Cosimo III, the use of the villa was granted to Violante of Bavaria, the widow of his eldest son, Grand Prince Ferdinando. For a brief period, she gathered artists and men of letters at the villa, collecting several important series of portraits. The villa was later neglected by the Lorraine dinasty and then sold in 1816 to the Capacci family.

Since that time the villa has been radically altered by the demolition of the top floor and the transformation of the gardens into farm land. The villa has changed hands since then (it was bought by the famous sculptor Giovanni Dupré in 1875), but has remained privately owned.

# Villa di Marignolle

The fourteenth-century 'gentleman's residence' on Marignolle hill was sold by the Sacchetti family to Lorenzo di Piero Ridolfi, from whom it was confiscated in 1559 by Francesco I, who accused Ridolfi of taking part in the anti-Medici plot ordered by Orazio Pucci.

The grand-duke Francesco I de' Medici commissioned Bernardo Buontalenti to restructure the villa and in 1587 he gave it to Don Antonio, his 'natural' son by Bianca Cappello. The only Medici property in this area on the outskirts of Florence, the elegant villa, which is now surrounded by ancient cypress trees, has hardly changed in appearance since it was designed by Buontalenti. The architect deviated here from his previous pattern of designing villas in adjoining blocks, as in, for example, Villa di Pratolino, and developed the single block of the building in a longitudinal direction. He arranged the villa on the summit of the hill with the façade towards Florence and balanced the two principal sides in harmonious, symmetrical forms.

In Utens' lunette, which, as always, faithfully reproduces even the smallest details, the villa is shown with white plaster work

**HOW TO GET THERE**

Leave the A1 motorway at Firenze Certosa and go on in the direction of Galluzzo. Continuing towards Florence on the via Senese, turn left into via delle Bagnese and right into via San Quirichino which leads directly into via di Marignolle. The villa is not open to the public.

The villa on the hill of Marignolle

103

## Don Antonio de' Medici

Don Antonio, the owner of Villa di Marignolle, is thought to be the offspring of the turbulent love affair between Francesco I de' Medici and Bianca Cappello. Married to the Florentine Pietro Buonaventuri, but soon the mistress of Grand-duke Cosimo's eldest son, who was married against his wish to Giovanna of Austria, this beautiful Venetian indissolubly bound Francesco I to herself in both life and death. A few years after they finally married, following the deaths of their respective spouses, they went to a hunt at Villa di Poggio a Caiano, where they died a few hours from one another on the 10 and 11 October 1587. Legend has it that they were poisoned by his brother, cardinal Ferdinando, who was anxious to seize power as the head of the Grand-duchy. According to legend, although Bianca Cappello asserted that Don Antonio was her son by Francesco, he was in fact the son of one of her servants. Once his uncle Ferdinando, who may have spread the rumour, was in power, he kept Don Antonio in regal style throughout his life.

and sandstone profiles, set above an embankment planted with trees and a lawn supported by a high plastered wall. The courtyard on the left (with the spacious room with large windows used for playing tennis, commissioned in 1596 by Don Antonio from the architect Gherardo Mechini), appears to be surrounded by a battlemented wall. The successful setting in the landscape was originally highlighted by the long perspective of the avenue which cut through wooded fields to the monumental gate at the foot of the hill.

In 1621 the villa and its farm were bought by Girolamo di Gino Capponi and remained in his family until Gino Capponi, the well-known man of letters and politician died in 1876; he was first buried in Marignolle Chapel and later moved to the Pantheon in Santa Croce.

Among later owners, mention should be made of marquis Luigi Ridolfi and, from 1939 to 1976, the Bellini antique dealers.

Above,
Justus Utens, *Villa di Marignolle,*
1599-1602; Florence, Museo storico
topografico 'Firenze com'era'

# Villa La Magia

The original part of the villa, in the Ombrone valley at the northern foot of Monte Albano, near Quarrata, was built during the 14th century by the Panciatichi family from Pistoia. A stone plaque above a door commemorates the meeting here during a hunting expedition between duke Alessandro de' Medici and the emperor Charles V.

The old castle and surrounding estate, bordering the Villa di Poggio a Caiano estate, were bought by Francesco I in 1583, as part of the dynasty's progressive expansion of its lands and property in the Grand-duchy.

The unusual position, connected to the group of hunting reserves (Poggio, Artimino, L'Ambrogiana and Montevettolini) that gravitated like satellites around the central hunting reserve of 'Barco Reale', set up by Cosimo I, made La Magia an exceptional place for hunting. In 1585 Bernardo Buontalenti was commissioned to restructure the villa as a hunting lodge, as can be seen in Utens' faithful representation, which shows a modest residence with the air of a simple country house.

The square plan villa is represented with a central courtyard

## HOW TO GET THERE

In the centre town of Quarrata.
*Address* via Vecchia Fiorentina 63, Quarrata (Pistoia). Currently closed for restoration, is shortly due to re-open.

The South front of the villa

Above, Justus Utens,
*Villa La Magia*,
1599-1602;
Florence, Museo
storico topografico
'Firenze com'era'

Right above,
the inner courtyard

and two projecting wings at the ends of the diagonal. It seems to have no garden and to be connected with the surrounding farms and woods only by means of straight roads. An unusual feature of the Pistoia villa was its large artificial lake (now lost) with walled banks, which was used for fishing and hunting aquatic birds, as the 'hut' in the centre of the lake, designed by Buontalenti and his assistant Davide Fortini, clearly shows. Work was completed in a very short period: at the end of 1585 Benedetto Uguccioni, the overseer of Grand-ducal works, informed Francesco that building work was completed at the villa except the paving of the inner courtyard and the raising of the pigeon house, which would be shortly finished.

Given by Ferdinando I to Francesco I's illegitimate son, Don Antonio de' Medici, the property was sold in 1645 by Ferdinando II to Pandolfo Attavanti, who transformed the hunting lodge into a villa with gardens arranged in parterres and fresco decoration by Giovan Domenico Ferretti (1715). In 1752 the villa was sold to the Ricasoli, who sold it in 1766 to the Amati, in whose hands it remained until it was recently sold to Quarrata Commune.

# Villa di Coltano

Coltano estate, near San Piero in Grado (Pisa), was originally owned by the monks of San Savino Abbey and assigned by papal bull in 1562 to the Order of the Knights of St Stephen. The land was reclaimed in 1558 by Cosimo I de' Medici who dug the 'Bocchette' channel during the general drainage of the marshes inland from Pisa and Livorno. The huge agricultural estate, with excellent grain production and livestock farming, produced vast quantities of dairy products and was admired by Michel de Montaigne during his visit in 1581.

Don Antonio, Francesco I and Bianca Cappello's illegitimate son, commissioned Bernardo Buontalenti to build the villa after 1586. Buontalenti's design for the villa, the management centre of the estate, included four corner towers and is typical of many of the Medici's fortified residences.

**HOW TO GET THERE**

From Florence take the carriageway Firenze-Pisa-Livorno and turn off at Pisa Aeroporto. From there join the Aurelia (SS 1) and follow to Coltano.
*Owner* Comune di Pisa
Visiting Centre – Ente Parco Migliarino San Rossore Massaciuccoli.
*Address* Via Palazzi, Tenuta di Coltano, Pisa.
Tel +39 050 989084
*Opening times* Mon-Fri 9-13 / 14-16; spring-summer open also Sat. and Sun.
*Entry* free.
Guided visits and activities related to the park.

The backside of the villa

Above,
the outer chapel

Right,
the main front
of the villa

Next page,
a *View of Coltano*
Florence, Archivio
di Stato

Used by the Grand-dukes as a hunting lodge, the villa and estate became one of the eight Grand-ducal hunting reserves, along with Poggio Imperiale, Cascine dell'Isola, Poggio a Caiano ('Barco Mediceo'), Cafaggiolo, Migliarino, San Rossore and Tombolo. After the end of the Medici line in 1737, the austere country villa passed into the hands of the Lorraine family and was trans-formed into an increasingly ostentatious villa, fit to receive illustrious guests and sovereigns: Ferdinando I Bourbon stayed here in 1785.

Once again used as a hunting reserve by Leopoldo II, it was given to the 'Opera Nazionale Combattenti' after the Unification of Italy along with much other Crown property. Today it is owned by Pisa Commune.

# Villa dell'Ambrogiana

## HOW TO GET THERE

In the centre town of Montelupo.
*Address* viale Umberto I 64, Montelupo (Florence).
It is currently home of a penitentiary.
*For information* +39 0571 518993.

The Medici bought a property from the Ambrogi, including a fishing lodge and estate, on the left bank of the Arno near the confluence with the Pesa, in 1574, the same year in which documents reveal that Bartolommeo Ammannati and his assistant Giovanni Antonio Dosio carried out work for Francesco I. The complete rebuilding, which was faithfully represented by Utens in a lunette, was begun by Ferdinando I in 1587, immediately upon his election as Grand-duke of Tuscany. The architectural design, in which the original fishing lodge was transformed into a large and comfortable residence, complete with everything from a landing stage to a lush garden, is traditionally attributed to Bernardo Buontalenti, although the only name known for certain is that of one of the architect's assistants, Raffaello Pagni, who oversaw the building work. The villa is traditional and does not offer

A perspective of the entrance of the villa

any novel architectural elements: the solid square plan, laid out around a large inner courtyard, with projecting towers at the corners and reinforced profiles, is another example of a villa-fortress, underlining the Prince's strong hold on the area. The garden is more innovative, also forming the entrance area to the villa as it includes the landing stage on the river: rigorously divided into four squares delimited by 'circles' of evergreen plants, it was decorated with a grotto, in a bank near the Arno, designed by Giovan Battista Ferrucci del Tadda.

On account of its unusual position on the banks of the most important water course in the region, and at the foot of the vast hunting reserve on Monte Albano, L'Ambrogiana soon became one of the villas most visited by the Medici Court, both as a resting place during frequent trips

A general view of the villa from the outside, with the four angular towers

## Cosimo III and the 'Science of the Nature'

The main entrance
stairway

In 1677 Cosimo built a loggia at L'Ambrogiana, to house the Cabinet of Natural History. The Grand-ducal doctor and naturalist, Francesco Redi carried out experiments on animals at the villa following the new Galilean experimentalism. The animals included rare species, such as a large Indian bird, the 'caracos', which was "brought to Grosseto beach by a south-westerly gale" as well as natural monstrosities such as a calf and sheep with two heads and a black stork; all the animals were painted by the court painter, Bartolomeo Bimbi.

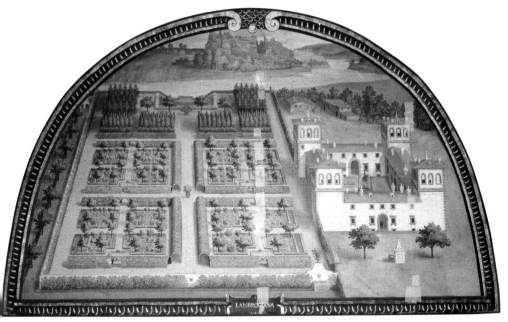

Left,
the East side of the villa

between Florence and Pisa, and as a place for amusement and rest in the intervals between hunting excursions, which followed on from each other as regularly as the seasons.

The villa was a favourite with Cosimo III, who amassed various painting, botanical and naturalistic collections here and commissioned Ferdinando Tacca to decorate the villa. He gave vent to his religious fervour near here

by building the Convent of San Pietro d'Alcantara, which housed a community of monks brought over from Spain.

Drastically changed during the 18th century, with the addition of a further floor and the modification of the façades, in the mid 19th century Leopoldo II transformed the villa into a mental asylum; it was later turned into a mental hospital for prisoners, and remains so to this day.

Above,
Justus Utens,
*Villa dell'Ambrogiana*,
1599-1602;
Florence, Museo storico topografico
'Firenze com'era'

Right above,
Giuseppe Zocchi,
*The Royal Villa dell'Ambrogiana*

113

# Villa di Artimino

**HOW TO GET THERE**

From Florence take the carriageway to Pisa-Livorno and turn off at Lastra a Signa; from there follow the signs for Artimino and go on for another 3 km up to the entrance for the villa.
*Owners* Artimino S.p.A.
*Address* viale papa Giovanni XXIII 1, Artimino – Carmignano (Prato). *Tel* +39 055 8751427/8/9
*Opening times* every Tue morning from 9 to 12 only by appointment. *Entry* free.
On the ground-floor the 'Museo Archeologico comunale di Artimino' can be visited (*opening times* open every Sunday 10-12; from February to October 9:30-12:30, closed Wed. *Entry* € 4,00 (full); € 2,00 (reduced).
*For information Tel* +39 055 8718124).

Baldinucci relates that while Ferdinando I was hunting in the 'Barco Reale' with Bernardo Buontalenti he stopped on a hill-top to rest and asked the aging architect to design a villa big enough to 'suffice' for him and his court and to be built as quickly as possible. Villa di Artimino, with its unique rooftop crowned by numerous chimneys, dominates the hill jutting out like a bastion from Monte Albano towards the narrow gully where the Arno is hemmed in by the Gonfolina outcrop. Completed in only four years, between 1596 and 1600, Villa di Artimino, or 'La Ferdinanda' as it is sometimes called, is both the masterpiece and the stylistic synthesis of Buon-talenti's mature period. As the famous architect was old, and travel difficult, he oversaw the building work from his Florentine house in Via Maggio, with the on site assistance of Santi Maiani and Gherardo Mechini. The imposing villa is fortress-like, with two long symmetrical façades with corner bastions – reaching to the roof on the side facing the country and to the *piano nobile* to create two terraces on the sides overlooking Florence. The hilltop villa enjoys panoramic views stretching from the Arno valley to the Pistoia plain and the Apuan Alps beyond: it is an ideal place from which to visually and symbolically admire the extent of the Grand-duchy. It was for this rea-

A view from the villa, with the 'Paggeria' (servants' quarters) on the right and the village of Artimino on the background

son that Cosimo commissioned the Flemish painter Justus Utens to paint the famous series of *Medici Villas* for Artimino, which was seen as the true fulcrum of the Medici Duchy. The paintings were placed in seventeen lunettes in a reception room on the *piano nobile*, known as the 'Villa Room', while an adjoining room, known as the 'War Room' was decorated with lunettes, now lost, representing battles.

Ferdinando, who considered Artimino his favourite summer residence, built an austere 'Guardaroba' (wardrobe) decorated with fine paintings, including *Pietro Aretino* by Titian and *Bacchus* by Caravaggio. He also commissioned Domenico Passignano and Bernardino Poccetti to decorate the Grand-ducal apartments,

Above,
the West front

Right above,
Domenico Cresti,
known as

Il Passignano,
*Allegory
of Happiness*, end
of the 16th century;
Villa di Artimino,
official room

Next page,
the frescoed
loggia
on the West front

115

the central hall, loggia and chapel with mythological scenes alluding to the virtues of the Medici. The western façade of the villa is dominated by a central loggia with four Doric columns. It is reached by a double staircase, built in 1930 by the architect Enrico Lusini to a design by Buontalenti. The original single flight of stairs, which it replaces, resembled a drawbridge and was much better suited to the archaic spirit of Buontalenti's Mannerism.

Equally incongruous is the containing wall below, which was built at the same time as the staircase in order to create a garden: it nullifies the direct relationship between the architecture and the surrounding countryside, which was intentionally adopted, with no mediation, at the villa.

The nearby 'Paggeria' (servants' quarters) is of great interest: the simple architecture of these buildings is characterised by a double tier of loggias.

The villa was sold in 1782 by Pietro Leopoldo of Lorraine to marquis Lorenzo Bartolomei who left it to his heirs, the Passerini counts, in 1848. In 1911 it was bought by the Maraini.

In the Autumn of 1944 Allied bombing severely damaged Artimino, which was restored by the architect Ferdinando Poggi within a short period from the Spring of 1945. Following further changes in ownership (the Riva family sold the property and auctioned furniture and paintings in 1979), the villa and surrounding buildings are now a congress centre and hotel complex. The basements of the villa house the Museo Archeologico comunale di Artimino.

## Justus Utens lunettes

The seventeen lunettes painted by Justus Utens (a Flemish artist who has been little studied) for the 'Villa Room' in Artimino were executed between 1599 and 1602. Removed from Artimino (the original site) at an unknown date, probably when the Lorraine sold the villa in 1782, they remained in the Grand-ducal collections until the fourteen extant lunettes were distributed between the Museo storico topografico 'Firenze com'era' and the Depositi (storerooms) of the Galleria Palatina. The lunettes represent the villas of Cafaggiolo, Trebbio, Poggio a Caiano, Castello, Seravezza, Pitti, La Petraia, Pratolino, L'Ambrogiana, La Magia, Marignolle, Montevettolini, Colle Salvetti and Lappeggi. The villas chosen by Ferdinando for the remaining three lunettes are not known, but it is likely that Villa di Artimino was among them.

# Villa di Montevettolini

Set on a high hill on the west slopes of Monte Albano, Villa di Montevettolini, or 'Monte Veturino' (as it is named in Justus Utens' lunette), was built after 1595 by Grand-duke Ferdinando I on the site of a pre-existing Medici property. Its position on the edge of the 'Barco Reale', the immense, walled hunting reserve which stretched from Poggio a Caiano to include the whole of Monte Albano, made it popular during the Medici Court's frequent hunting expeditions. The architect Gherardo Mechini was commissioned to restructure the building with the help of Domenico Marcacci of Pistoia. Older buildings, including a fort and a stretch of wall in the hamlet dating to the Republican era, were incorporated into the polygonal-plan villa. The imposing, severe fortress-like appearance of the villa was underlined by the barbican reinforcements of the foundations, the small windows and the observation sentry-boxes on the corners.

The position of the villa, with two sides rising almost vertically from

**HOW TO GET THERE**

From Florence take the A11 motorway (Firenze-Mare) as far as the turn-off for Montecatini Terme. From there go on in the direction of Monsummano Terme until Montevettolini. The villa is not open to the public.

A view of the villa from the outside.

117

Justus Utens,
*Villa di Monte
Veturino,*
1599-1602;
Florence, Museo
storico topografico
'Firenze com'era'

The entrance
of the villa
from the village

the valley below, also contributed to the sense of a defensive building, as can be seen in Justus Utens' lunette. The villa almost seems to be an avant-corps of the hamlet behind, which is distinguished by the Romanesque bell tower of the Parish church of San Michele Arcangelo.

Despite its appearance, the villa was the administrative centre for the vast estates in the Lower Valdinievole and was principally a place for rest and pleasure, as Utens showed by the many chimneys on the roof, the two walled vegetable gardens with fruit trees, and at the rear, a large terraced garden with geometrical parterres. Ferdinando I visited the villa over a long period, both during hunting expeditions and while travelling to check on the family's land in the reclaimed areas extending from Pieve a Nievole to Fucecchio marsh, which he had drained in order to increase Medici properties with the Grand-ducal farms at Ponte a Cappiano, Montevettolini, Bellavista, Castelmartini, Altopascio and Terzo.

Ferdinando II did not share the same interests and sold the villa, with most of the surrounding land on 17 August 1650. The estate then passed to the Bartolommei family, who owned it until 1871, when it was sold to prince Marcantonio Borghese, who carried out extensive renovation to the villa, which had been radically changed in the past, in order to restore it to its sixteenth-century appearance.

It is still owned by the Borghese family.

# Villa di Poggio Imperiale

In 1565 Cosimo I de' Medici confiscated the old fortified residence on Arcetri hill (known as Poggio Baroncelli after the original owners), from the Salviati, who had bought it in 1548, in retaliation for the anti Medici attitude of Alessandro Salviati. Given by Cosimo to his daughter Isabella, wife of the duke of Bracciano, Paolo Giordano Orsini, it passed after her death (she was killed by her husband in Villa di Cerreto Guidi in 1576), to her son Don Virginio Orsini. Inherited by Maria Maddalena of Austria, wife of Grand-duke Cosimo III, the estate was enlarged and the original 'gentleman's residence' was entirely restructured between 1622 and 1625 to designs by the architect Giulio Parigi. The designs enlarged the existing building to the east and added a new, airy façade, crowned by a roof-terrace and closed by two low, terraced wings. A semicircular balustrade decorated with statues linked the two wings to form a wide semi-circle on the lawn in front of the villa, which was used for outdoor theatrical productions. Of great importance for the novelty in urban planning, linking the villa with the town, and at the same time projecting the town into the surrounding countryside, was the functional, monumental, straight avenue which cut down Monticelli hill to connect Poggio Imperiale with Porta Romana (formerly Porta San Piero Gattolini). Sided by dense cypress woods, there were originally four imposing fish ponds with sculpture and heraldic insignia (removed in 1773) at the bottom of the avenue. The theatricality of Parigi's architecture and the numerous gardens at Villa di Poggio Imperiale

**HOW TO GET THERE**

From Porta Romana, not far from Piazzale Michelangelo. *Address* piazzale del Poggio Imperiale, Florence. *Bus* 11 *Tel* +39 055 226171 *Opening times* visits only by appointment; closed August. *Entry* free.

The monumental façade of the villa

The Villa di Poggio
Imperiale
in a fresco
by anonymous
inside the 'Room of
the Hearings', detail

*Darting Jove,*
by Felice Palma
(17th century)
and *Hercules
bearing
the heavens,*
by Vincenzo de'
Rossi (16th century)

was equalled by the contemporary decoration in the apartments of Maria Maddalena and her son Ferdinando, executed by Matteo Rosselli and his assistants. The important frescoes at Poggio Imperiale (known by this name from 1624 in reference to the illustrious birth of the Grand-duchess), are in a perfect state of conservation; they reflect the religious fervour of the patron, with the subjects celebrating both the House of Austria (in stories of kings and emperors defending orthodox faith), and illustrious Christian women (in episodes from the lives of Biblical characters, saints and queens). The villa was bought in 1659 by the wife of Ferdinando II, Vittoria della Rovere, and further enlargements were made, to designs by Giacinto Maria Marmi, between 1681 and 1683. It

of Ferdinando III, surmounting the newly-built central portico with a tympanum loggia with five arches and an internal peristyle,

A close-up detail of a paper hanging made in China in the 18th century

was under the Lorraine family that this prestigious suburban villa, convenient for the Grand-dukes' Summer and Autumn holidays, was embellished. Pietro Leopoldo commissioned Gaspero Paoletti to carry out the large-scale renovation work between 1766 and 1783. Work concentrated on the two inner courtyards in place of the original walled gardens, the new stables, and above all the general redecoration of numerous rooms, ornamented with fine stucco work by the Ticinese Grato and Giocondo Albertolli, maritime views by Antonio Cioci, gallant scenes by Gesualdo Ferri and Chinese and Indian wall paper and fabrics imported from the East. The Neo-classical transformation of the façade was completed later by Pasquale Poccianti for the queen of Etruria, Maria Luisa Borbone, who inherited the villa in Napoleonic times. In 1807, the new Grand-duchess, Elisa Baciocchi commissioned Giuseppe Cacialli to complete the design projects during the restoration

and substituting the two baroque wings with two massive porticoed buildings. The building to the left held the Chapel, decorated with a painting by Francesco Nenci in the vault, stucco work by Bertel Thorwaldsen and with sculpture by Francesco Carradori and Stefano Ricci.
After the Unification of Italy and with the transferral of the Capital to Florence, the villa was taken over by the SS. Annunziata boarding School (1865), and it remains a school to this day.

General view of the villa fron the facing square

121

# Index of names

## A

Acuto, Giovanni 16
Alberti, Leon Battista 8, 73
Albertolli, Giocondo 121
Albertolli, Grato 121
Allori, Alessandro 10, 46, 53, 63
  *Consul Flaminio speaking to the council of the Acheans (The)* 53
  *Hercules and the Good Fortune guarding the Garden of the Hesperides* 63
  *Syphax King of Numidia receiving Scipio* 53
Altissimo, Cristoforo dell' 54
Amati (family) 106
Ambrogi (family) 110
Ammannati, Bartolomeo 27, 33, 35, 38, 39, 41, 92, 97, 110
  *Apennines (The)* 33, 41, *41*
  *Hercules raising Anteus* 27, *35*, 38
  *Mounts Senario and Falterona* 33
  *Mugnone river with Fiesole and the Arno river (The)* 33
Ammirato, Scipione 90
  *Storie Fiorentine* 90
Andrea del Sarto 24, 45, 53, 63
  *Holy Family* 24
  *Tribute to Caesar (The)* 53
Anna of Austria 51
Aretino, Pietro 115
Asselt, Jacob Eber van 64
Attavanti, Pandolfo 106

## B

Baciocchi, Elisa 21, 48, 50, 55, 121
Baldi, Niccolò 78
Baldinucci (family) 114
Bandini, Giovanni 86, 87
  *Hercules killing the Hydra* 86, 87, *87*
Bardi (family) 100
Bardini, Stefano 64
Bardini, Ugo 64
Baroncelli (family) 119
Bartolini Salimbeni 100
Bartolomei (family) 118
Bartolomei, Lorenzo 116
Bavaria, Violante Beatrice of 102
Beaubrun, Charles e Henry 26
*Henrietta of England duchess of Orléans* 26
Bellini (family) 104
Belon, Pierre 34
Bertoldo 52
and Sansovino, Andrea, Sangallo, Andrea, *Frieze* 52, (details) *52-53*
Bimbi, Bartolomeo 56, 91, 112
  *Cherries 56*
Boldrini, Galliano 61
Borghese (family) 74, 118
Borghese, Marcantonio 118
Borghini, Vincenzo 46
Botti, Matteo 87
Botti, Rinaldo 19, 24, 101
Botticelli, Sandro 34, 85

*Birth of Venus* 34
*Spring* 34
Bourbon, Ferdinando I de 108
Bourbon, Marie Luise de 48, 121
Bronzino, Agnolo, 76
Brunelleschi (family) 16
Brunelleschi, Filippo 44, 75
Bruschi, Alberto 62
Buonaventuri, Pietro 104
Buontalenti, Bernardo 18, 34, 60, 61, 92, 95, 97, 99, 100, 103, 105, 106, 107, 110, 114, 116

## C

Cacialli, Giuseppe 55, 121
Capacci (family) 102
Cappello, Bianca 46, 50, 93, 98, 103, 104, 107
Capponi, Gino 104
Capponi, Girolamo 104
Caravaggio, Michelangelo Merisi known as 115
  *Bacchus* 115
Carradori, Francesco 121
Carucci, Jacopo *see* Pontormo
Casini (family) 65
Casini, Valore 63
Cassani, Niccolò 11
  *The Grand Prince Ferdinando de' Medici (detail) 11*
Cataneo, Pietro G. 60
  *I quattro primi libri di architettura* 60
Catani, Luigi 48, 50, 51, 55
  *Apollo and Minerva* 50, *50*
  *Lorenzo the Magnificent receiving the model of the villa from Giuliano da Sangallo and Angelo Poliziano crowning the bust of Homer with laurel* 51
Charles V 23, 76, 105
Cioci, Antonio 121
Cioli, Valerio 98
Clement VII 23, 54, 76
Conti, Antonio 64
Corsini (family) 85
Corsini, Bartolomeo 85
Cresti, Domenico *see* Passignano, Domenico
Croci, Domenico Frilli 27
  *Rinaldo in the garden of Armida* 27
Curradi, Francesco 27
  *Artemisia* 27
  *Erminia among the shepherds* 27
Cutting, Sybil 81
Cybo Malaspina (family) 83
Cybo, Francesco 85

## D

Daddi, Cosimo 19, 23
*Exploits of Goffredo of Buglion at the taking of Jerusalem* 19, 22
*Glory of the Holy Spirit among Angels and Elect* 27

Dandini, Pier 19, 24, 99, 101
Dante da Castiglione 76
Danti, Vincenzo 98
Della Stufa (family) 30
Demidoff (family) 97, 98
Doccia 24, 24
Donatello 75, 79
Dosio, Giovanni Antonio 110
Dupré, Giovanni 102

## E

Eleonora of Toledo 82
Emanuele of Mirafiori 21, 23
Henrietta of England duchess of Orléans 26
Este (family) 83
Este, Maria Beatrice d' 83

## F

Fagiuoli, Giovan Battista 101
Frederick IV King of Denmark and Norway 102
Feltrini, Andrea di Cosimo 52
  decoration in the Leo X Room *52*
Ferretti, Giovan Domenico 106
Ferri (family) 50
Ferri, Antonio 99, 101
Ferri, Gesualdo 121
Ferrucci, Giovan Battista del Tadda 111
Fevére, Pietro 64
Ficino, Marsilio 52, 73, 75
Philip IV of Spain 51
Focardi, Ruggero 61
Foggini, Giovan Battista 97
  *Dragon* 97
Fortini, Davide 16, 34, 94, 106
Fortuni, David 60
Franceschini, Baldassarre *see* Volterrano
Francesco di Cristofano *see* Franciabigio
Francis I of France 22
Franciabigio 45, 53, 55
  *Return of Cicero from exile* 53, *54*
Fratellini, Giovanna 26
Frietsch, Joseph 20, 29, 97
Fummo, Achille di Napoli 24
  Piano-harmonium 24
Furttenbach, Joseph 34

## G

Gabbiani, Anton Domenico 46, 53, 99
  *Apotheosys of Cosimo* 46, 53
Galli, Ferdinando da Bibbiena 99
Gattolini, Piero san 119
Geddes da Filicaja (family) 61, 63
Gherardini, Alessandro 101
Ghirlandaio, Domenico 85
  *Storiy of Vulcan* 85
Giambologna 9, 19, 20, 22, 25, 27, 29, 33, 39, 95, 96, 97

*Apennines 95*, 96, (detail) *96*, 97
*Cosimo I de' Medici* (detail) *9*
*Mugnone 96*
*Venere Fiorenza 19*, 20, 22, 25, 27, 29, 33
Giardi, Giuseppe 21
Giovanna of Austria 104
Giovanni da San Giovanni 19
Giovio, Paolo 45
Goffredo of Buglion 19, 22
Gondi, Giuliano 87
Gonzaga, Eleonora 102
González, Bartolomé 51
Gualtierotti (family) 100
Guidi (family) 58

H

Hahn, Maximilian 83
Hapsburg Lorraine (family) 47, 60
Hapsburg Lorraine, Ferdinando
Carlo 83
Hapsburg Lorraine, Ferdinando III 65
Hapsburg Lorraine, Francesco
Ferdinando 83
Hugford, Ignazio 26
*Bacchanal 26*

K

Knights of the Monte 84
Knights of Altopascio 84

L

Landino, Cristoforo 81
Larderel, Blanche de 23
Lasinio, Ferdinando 21, 25, 29
Leo X 19, 22, 45, 46, 52, 53, 54, 73
Leopoldo II 20, 108, 113
Lepaute 24
*Gilt bronze clock 24*
Lippi, Filippino 45, 85
*The sacrifice of Laocoon 45*
Lippi, Filippo 79
Lippi, Tommaso 75
Lisippo 28, 40
*Apoxyómenos 28, 40*
Lorenzi, Antonio 39
Lorenzo da Castiglione 76
Lorraine (family) 10, 19, 27, 41, 74, 77, 91, 93, 94, 102, 108, 121
Lorrraine, Carlo II of 27
Lorraine, Cristina of 19, 34, 93
Lorraine, Ferdinando III of 10, 20, 47, 97, 99, 121
Lorraine, Francesco II of 87
Lorraine, Francesco Stefano of 47
Lorraine, Pietro Leopoldo of 20, 28, 50, 65, 116 121
Lusini, Enrico 116

M

Maggi (family) 60, 65
Magnasco, Alessandro 28
Maiani, Santi 114
Malaspina, Alberigo Cybo 85
Maraini (family) 116
Marcacci, Domenico 117
Maria Maddalena of Austria 34, 54, 119
Marmi, Giacinto Maria 121
Martinotti (family) 51
Mazzini Marchi (family) 81

Mechini, Gherardo 56, 104, 114, 117
Medici (family) 8, 11, 34, 35, 63, 64, 69, 70, 73, 76, 78, 81, 84, 87, 91, 94, 107, 110
Medici, Alessandro de' 22, 70, 75, 76, 86, 94, 105
Medici, don Antonio de' 100, 103, 104, 106, 107
Medici, Caterina de' 22
Medici, Claudia de' 26
Medici, Cosimo de', known as the Elder 53, 68, 69, 71, 75, 78, 82
Medici, Cosimo I de', grand duke 9, 16, 23, 30, 32, 34, 39, 40, 46, 58, 65, 70, 73, 82, 86, 87, 90, 92, 94, 95, 104, 107, 119
Medici, Cosimo II de', grand duke 23, 34, 63, 87
Medici, Cosimo III de', grand duke 10, 11, 19, 24, 34, 41, 46, 54, 81, 90, 101, 91, 99, 102, 112, 113, 119
Medici, Ferdinando de', grand prince 10, 11, 46, 99, 102
Medici, Ferdinando I de', cardinal and grand duke 8, 9, 10, 16, 18, 19, 34, 46, 70, 74, 77, 82, 93, 94, 100, 104, 106, 110, 114,115, 118
Medici, Ferdinando II 54, 70, 87, 100, 106, 118, 120
Medici, don Francesco de' 65
Medici, Francesco I de' 9, 18, 23, 46, 50, 74, 93, 95, 96, 98, 100, 103, 104, 105, 106, 107, 110
Medici, Francesco Maria de', cardinal 9, 101, 102
Medici, Gian Gastone de' 46, 70
Medici, Giovan Carlo de', cardinal 9, 10, 26, 34, 77
Medici, Giovanni de' *see* Leo X
Medici, Giovanni di Bicci de' 68, 70, 75
Medici, Giovanni de', known as
Giovanni dalle Bande Nere 30, 70
Medici, Giovanni di Pierfrancesco
de' 30
Medici, don Giovanni de' 60
Medici, Giuliano de', duke of
Nemours 22, 45, 76
Medici, Giulio de' *see* Clemente VII
Medici, Ippolito de' 76
Medici, Isabella de' 64, 119
Medici, Leopoldo de', cardinal 60
Medici, don Lorenzo de' 10, 19, 34, 60, 94
Medici, Lorenzo de', duke of Urbino 23, 45, 76
Medici, Lorenzo di Pierfrancesco de' 30
Medici, Lorenzo de' known as the
Magnificent 8, 9, 42, 43, 44, 45, 46, 51, 52, 53, 70, 73, 75, 79, 83, 84, 85
*Ambra 43*
*Nencia da Barberino 73*
Medici, Maria de' 23
Medici, Maria Maddalena de' 27, 120
Medici, don Mattias de' 100
Medici, Pierfrancesco de' 30, 70
Medici, Piero de' 45, 53, 83, 85
Medici, don Pietro de' 60, 94
Melissi, Agostino 23
*Cosimo II recieveng the homage of
the Senate 23*
Michelangelo 19, 32,
*Brutus 19*

Michelozzo di Bartolomeo 44, 68, 69, 71, 75, 78
Mignani, Daniela 63
Montaigne, Michel de 34, 107

N

Nenci, Francesco 121
Niccolini (family) 89
Niccolini, Filippo 87
Niccolini, Giovan Luca 88
Nottolini, Lorenzo 26
Nuti, Fabio 21

O

Onofri, Crescenzio 28, 99
*Landscape with wayfarers 28*
Orford, lady 81
Orléans, Marguerite Louise d' 46, 50
Orsi, Vincenzo 77
Orsini, Francesco Cybo 83
Orsini, Giovanni Antonio 100
Orsini, Innocenzo cardinal 83
Orsini, Paolo Giordano 64, 119
Orsini, don Virginio 119

P

Pagni, Raffaello 18, 110
Palla Strozzi 16
Palma, Felice 120
*Darting Jove120*
Panciatichi (family) 105
Paoletti, Niccolò Gaspero 81, 121
Parigi, Alfonso the Elder 60
Parigi, Giulio 119
Passerini (family) 116
Passignano, Domenico 115,
*Allegoriy of Happiness 115*
*Amphinoi on the Dolphin 27*
Pazzi, Francesco de' 79
Pazzi, Jacopo de' 79
Perugino, Pietro 85
Petit, Jacob 52
*Alpine Landscapes 51*
*Pots-purris 51*
Pico della Mirandola 73, 80
Pieratti, Domenico 28
*Gladiators 22, 28, 35, 40*
Pierino da Vinci 28, 29
e Tribolo Niccolò, *Fountain Of
Hercules and Anteus 22, 33, 35, 36,
38*
*Fountain Fiorenza 20, 25, 29, 33, 35*
Piero da San Casciano 32
Piero the Gouty 75
Pinsent, Cecil 81
Florentine painter from the circle of
Alessandro Allori 10
*Cardinal e grand duke Ferdinando I
de' Medici* (detail) *10*
Poccetti, Bernardino 19, 27, 116
*Saints e Episodes from the life of
Christ and of saints 26-27*
Poccianti, Paquale 48, 51, 57, 121
Podestà, Girolamo 27
Poggi, Ferdinando 116
Poggini, Domenico 9
*Francesco I de' Medici* (detail) *9*
Poliziano, Agnolo 51, 52, 73, 81
Pollaiolo, Simone known as Il
Cronaca 85
Pontormo, Jacopo 7, 34, 45, 53, 75
*Return of the Golden Age 34*

*Vertumnus and Pomona* (detail) 6, 53, *54*
Prince of Craon 19
Pucci, Orazio 103

R

Raphael 27
   *Madonna of the Impannata* 27
Redi, Francesco 112
Riario, Raffaello 79
Ricasoli (family) 100, 106
Ricci, Sebastiano 46, 99
Ricci, Stefano 121
Ridolfi, Lorenzo di Piero 103
Ridolfi, Luigi 104
Riva (family) 116
Rosselli, Matteo 26, 27, 63, 120
   *Angelica and Medoro* 26
   *Saint Barbara* 63
   *Semiramis* 27
*Tancredi tended by Erminia and Vafrino* 26
Rossi, Vincenzo de' 120
   *Hercules bearing the Heavens* 120
Rovere, Vittoria della 54, 120-121
Rucellai, Giovanni 43
Ruggeri, Giovan Battista 46, 47, 57
Ruggeri, Giuseppe 46, 47
Rustici, Francesco 27
*Olindo and Sofronia freed by Clorinda* 27

S

Sacchetti (family) 103
Sailer, Antonio 49
Salutati (family) 16
Salvetti (family) 82
Salviati (family) 119
Salviati, Alessandro 119
Salviati, Francesco 79
Salviati, Maria 30, 70
Sangallo, Andrea da 44, 52
and Sansovino, Andrea, Bertoldo, *Frieze* 52, details*52-53*
Sangallo, Giovan Battista da 83
Sangallo, Giuliano da 43, 51
Sansovino, Andrea 52
and Sangallo, Andrea, Bertoldo, *Frieze* 52, details*52-53*
Savoia (family) 21, 36, 37, 49, 50, 53, Scaretti (family) 70
Sera, Cosimo del 81
Serragli, Giuliano 70
Sixtus IV pope 79
Sloane, Francis Joseph 77
Socci, Giovanni 20, 26
   *Table-desk* 20
Soderini (family) 94
Spence, William 81
Stradano, Giovanni 46, 64
   *Hunts* 64
Sustermans, Justus 11, 26
   *Claudia de' Medici* 26
   *Portrait of Cosimo III* (detail) *11*

T

Tacca, Ferdinando 113
Tadini, Buoninsegni Tobler (family) 83

Thorwaldsen, Bertel 121
Titian 115
   *Pietro Aretino* 115
Tobler, Oscar 83
Tonini (family) 60
Tornabuoni, Lucrezia 84
Tribolo, Niccolò 25, 28, 29, 32, 34, 35, 39, 46, 57, 60, 94 and Pierino da Vinci, *Fountain Of Hercules and Anteus* 22, 33, 35, 36, 38 *Fountain Fiorenza* 20, 25, 29, 33, 35 *Grotto of the Animals*38, *39*

U

Uguccioni, Benedetto 95, 106
Utens, Justus 8, 9, 18, 32, 34, 44, 46, 68, 70, 72, 73, 74, 82, 92, 93, 96, 98, 100, 104, 105, 106, 110, 113, 115, 116, 118
   *Il Trebbio* 68
   lunettes of *Medici Villas* 8, 18, 115, 116
*Villa dell'Ambrogiana 113*
*Villa di Cafaggiolo 72*
*Villa di Castello 32*
*Villa di Collesalvetti 82*
*Villa di Marignolle 104*
*Villa di Monte Veturino 118*
*Villa di Poggio a Caiano 44*
*Villa di Pratolino 98*
*Villa di Serravezza 92, 93*
*Villa La Magia 105, 106*
*Villa La Peggio 100*
*Villa La Petraia 18*

V

Varchi, Benedetto 32, 90
   *Storie Fiorentine* 90
Vasari, Giorgio 8, 32, 34, 39, 68, 73, 78, 85
   *Portrait of Lorenzo de' Medici* 8
Vercellana, Rosa 20, 21, 23, 25, 48, 54, 55
Verino, Michele 42, 52
Veronese, Paolo 50
   *The crossing of Red Sea* 50
   *Moses and the burning bush* 50
Villa del Tombolo 108
Villa del Trebbio 14, 68, 78, 116
Villa dell'Ambrogiana 9, 10, 14, 56, 87, 105, 110, 111, 112, 116
Villa della Topaia 12, 35, 90
Villa delle Cascine dell'Isola 108
Villa di Agnano 14, 83, 84
Villa di Artimino known as "Ferdinanda" 8, 9, 12, 18, 46, 77, 82, 105, 114, 115, 116
Villa di Cafaggiolo 14, 68, 71, 78, 108, 116
Villa di Camugliano 14, 86, 87
Villa di Careggi 9, 10, 12, 75, 76, 78, 79
Villa di Castello known as "l'Olmo" or "il Vivaio" 9, 10, 12, 19, 20, 22, 25, 27, 28, 29, 30, 32, 37, 45-46, 56, 90, 116
Villa di Castelmartini 77
Villa di Cerreto Guidi 10, 14, 58, 77,

94, 119
Villa di Collesalvetti 14, 82, 116
Villa di Coltano 14, 107
Villa di Lappeggi 9, 12, 100, 101, 116
Villa di Marignolle 12, 103, 104, 116
Villa di Marlia 20, 24, 26
Villa di Migliarino 108
Villa di Montevettolini 14, 105, 116, 117
Villa di Poggio a Caiano 10, 12, 19, 20, 21, 26, 42, 46, 56, 104, 105, 108, 116
Villa di Poggio Imperiale 12, 20, 108, 119, 120
Villa di Pratolino 9, 10, 12, 95, 101, 103, 116
Villa di Seravezza 14, 92, 116
Villa di Spedaletto 14, 83, 84, 85
Villa di Stabbia 14, 94
Villa La Magia 14, 105, 116
Villa La Petraia 9, 10, 16, 17, 18, 19, 20, 22, 24, 25, 28, 35, 36, 37, 40, 90, 116
Villa La Quiete 11
Villa La Topaia known as Cosmiano 10, 12, 56, 90
Villa Medici in Fiesole 12, 78, 79
Villa Medici sul Pincio 16
Villa Mezzomonte 11
Villa di Pratolino 95, 97
Villani, Giovanni 75
Vinne, Leonardo van der 27
Vittorio Emanuele II 20, 21, 23, 48, 50, 51, 54, 55
Vittorio Emanuele III 91
Volterrano 10, 19, 23, 34
   *Alessandro I duke of Firenze* 23
   *Caterina de' Medici with her children* 22
   *Clement VII crowns Charles V in Bologna* 23
   *Cosimo I takes his son Francesco into government* 23
   *Cosimo II receiving the victors of the venture of Bona* 22-23
   *Fasti medicei* 19, 22
   *Giuliano duke of Nemours and Lorenzo duke of Urbino on the Capitoline* 22
   *Tuscany's mastery of the Sea* 2"
   *The meeting beetween the pope Leo X e Francis I of France* 22
   *The triumphal entry of Cosimo I in Siena* 22
   *Maria de' Medici queen of France with her children* 23
   *Portrait of Giovan Carlo de' Medici* (detail) *10*
   *Wake and Sleep (The)* 34

Y

Youf, Jean-Baptiste Gilles 20, 26
   *Empire toilette* 20

Z

Zocchi, Giuseppe 60, 102, 113
   *The Royal Villa dell'Ambrogiana 113*
   *The Royal Vlla di Cerreto 60*
   *The Royal Villa di Lappeggi 102*

# Bibliographic references

G. Vasari, *Lives of the Most Eminent Painters, Sculptors, and Architects* (1568), translation by G. C. Du Vere (1912-1915), New York 1976

M. de Montaigne, *Journal de voyage en Italie par la Suisse et l'Allemagne en 1580 et 1581*, ed. by M. Rat, Paris 1955

G. Zocchi, *Vedute di Firenze e della Toscana* (1744), ed. by R. M. Mason, Firenze 1981

D. Moreni, *Notizie istoriche dei contorni di Firenze*, Firenze 1791-1795

E. Repetti, *Dizionario geografico-fisico-storico della Toscana*, Firenze 1833-1846

G. Carocci, *I dintorni di Firenze*, Firenze 1906-1907

G. Pieraccini, *La stirpe dei Medici di Cafaggiolo*, Firenze 1924

G. Lensi Orlandi, *Le ville di Firenze*, Firenze 1954

H. Acton, *Tuscan Villas*, London 1973

*Città, ville e fortezze della Toscana nel XVIII secolo*, ed. by

A. Fara, C. Conforti, L. Zangheri, Firenze 1978

V. Franchetti Pardo, G. Casali, *I Medici nel contado fiorentino. Ville e possedimenti agricoli tra quattrocento e cinquecento*, Firenze 1978

L. Zangheri, *Pratolino il giardino delle meraviglie*, Firenze 1979

*Luoghi della Toscana medicea*, ed. by A. Godoli, A. Natali, Firenze 1980

D. Mignani, *Le Ville Medicee di Giusto Utens*, Firenze 1980

L. Zangheri, *Ville della provincia di Firenze. La città*, Firenze 1989

E. Cassarino, *La villa medicea di Artimino*, Firenze 1990

C. Acidini Luchinat, G. Galletti, *Le Ville e i Giardini di Castello e Petraia*, Pisa 1992

C. Cresti, *Civiltà delle ville toscane*, Udine 1992

P. E. Foster, *La Villa di Lorenzo de' Medici a Poggio a Caiano*, Pisa 1992

P. Grifoni, D. Mignani, F. Nannelli, *La villa medicea di Cerreto Guidi*, Firenze 1993

M. Azzi Visentini, *La villa in Italia Quattrocento e Cinquecento*, Milano 1995

F. Faini, A. M. Puntri, *La villa mediceo lorenese del Poggio Imperiale*, Firenze 1995

O. Guaita, *Ville e giardini storici in Italia*, Milano 1995

*Giardini medicei*, ed. by C. Acidini Luchinat, Milano 1996

O. Guaita, *Le ville della Toscana*, Roma 1997

C. Barni, *Villa La Magia. Una dimora signorile nel contado pistoiese (secc. XIV-XIX)*, Firenze 1999

*La Villa di Marignolle da Franco Sacchetti a Gino Capponi*, ed. by M. Seidel, Venezia 2000

*La Villa Medicea di Poggio a Caiano*, Livorno 2000

M. Pozzana, *Gardens of Florence and Tuscany. A complete guide*, Firenze 2001

To the following pages,
the Villa di Careggi